ALSO BY JAMES L. HARTER, SR.

Mindsongs: Chapter One
Heartfelt Thoughts: Chapters Two & Three
Mindsongs/Treks
Mindsongs/Strolling
Heartfelt Thoughts: Chapters Four & Five
Mindsongs/Wayfarer
Lovesongs
Heartfelt Thoughts: Chapters Six & Seven
Preface to Life
Life Goes on
Heartfelt Thoughts: Chapters Eight & Nine
Glimpses of Life
Catching Up
Heartfelt Thoughts: Chapters Ten & Eleven
Seek   Find
On, on Moving On
Heartfelt Thoughts: Chapters Twelve & Thirteen
Up, up and away
Here Now and Ever After
Heartfelt Thoughts: Chapters Fourteen thru Sixteen
Envisioning the Future
Believing
Tomorrow's Dawn

The Good Times Party Songbook
BY B. BURBUS
(Unpublished)

Heartfelt Thoughts

Chapters Fourteen thru Sixteen

James L. Harter Sr.

Heartfelt Thoughts Chapters Fourteen thru Sixteen - James L. Harter Sr.
Copyright © 2017 by James L. Harter Sr.
Heartfelt Thoughts Chapters Fourteen thru Sixteen - James L. Harter Sr.
166p. ill. cm.
ISBN 978-1-935795-06-3
_____

All Rights Reserved. No part of this book may be reproduced, stored in a retrieval system, or transmitted in any form or by any means, electronic, mechanical, photocopying, recording, or otherwise, without permission in writing from MRK Publishing

MRK Publishing
PO Box 353431
Palm Coast, FL 32135-3431
Printed in the United States of America

I would like to dedicate to all my friends and family; those memories of days of both happiness and sadness that we may have shared on our journeys throughout our lives.

Yet, who may we meet when we awake tomorrow?

"To realize our true destiny, we must be guided not by a myth from our past, but by a vision of our future."
-Mark B. Adams, discussing
The visionary biology of J.B.S. Haldane

CONTENTS
Chapter Fourteen: Envisioning the Future

Preface   2
Breathe   5
Hiawatha's Hiatus   6
The Garden of Vegan   6
Rhyme Surfing   9
Flutter   10
Augmenting Angst   11
Flow   13
Circles   13
The Dunce in the Corner   14
Omens Imaged   16
Idle Hours   17
Move and Shake   18
Softly Falls the Light of Day   18
The Start of Something Big   19
Alma Mater Avalanche   22
Where am I going?   23
Unfound   23
Just Three Little Words   24
The Horizontal Lab   25
Wannabes   26
Transformer   27
Together   28
Reign Refrain   28
Stuck Up   29
Moon Halo   29
Clan-destiny   30
Sometimes in Rhyme   31
Dream Building Team   32
Tirades on a Rampage   33
Nightlight   35

End Times   35
Until   36
Couplet Capers   37
Scrapbook Snapshots   38
Emotional Game   42
Lonely Hearts Club   43
Nit-picking Nonsense   44
Conversing with One's Self   44
Scramble   45
Curiosity   46
Visiting Cities   50
Being Shy   51
Parting Ways   52
Adrift   52
Carefree   53
Rising   53
Resemblance   54
Milligan's Lament   55
Redundancy   56
In a Jaded Jungle   57
Scissor- Hands   57
Star-struck   58
Engaging Likeness   59
How it Ends   60
Autumn Twilight   61
Have you heard?   61
Of Pine Barrens   62
Oath Renewal   62
Genesis   63
Souls in Motion   63
How Novel   68
Creeping Out   69
The Beginning   70

Chapter Fifteen: Believing
Preface   73
Escape   74
Crank It Up   74
All in the Family   75
The Bits and Pieces   75
Waves of Light   78
Free Reign   78
About Writing   79
Black Cloud Saloon at Thunder Gulch:
     A Tale of Yore   80
The First Anomaly   84
The Second Anomaly   85
Play by Play   86
All about Ells   86
A Solemn Vow   87
Flights of Fire   87
Bred Crumbs   88
Off His Rocker; Out to Lunch   88
Tale of Two Ditties: One Ditty One
              Two Ditty Two   89
The Shopkeeper   90
The Beginning   93

Chapter Sixteen: Tomorrow's Dawn
Preface   96
Dawn   97
Coming from the Dark Side   98
Cat Scanners   99
Lost in Conversation   99
Tiger Lily   100
Thru a Looking Glass   100
Creation   101

Poetry of Life   101
There is Always More to Learn   103
Zero   103
Lonesome Trail   104
Here lies the Land of Ever   105
Avenue of Dreams   106
Battle of Poetic Wits   107
Picture This in Song   107
The Come-ons   108
Star in My Pocket   109
Liquid Mind   110
Clairvoyant Insight   110
Transcendent Tendency   111
The Arrival   112
Remember   112
Drifting   113
Trendsetting   114
Captain Marvel   114
Danger Lurks   115
Another Time   115
Short Snorts   115
The Fifth of Four   115
Little Big Pause   116
Vendetta   116
To Amuse a Muse   117
The Feather and the Fern   118
The Genesis Conundrum   120
Changing of the Guard   121
Breaking News   122
Life of Day   123
Three Times a Lady   124
Warped Wit   125
Contemplation of the Little Things   126

Odds-on Favorite   127
Buckets of Charm   128
Impact   129
A Nutty Anecdote   129
What's Brewing?   130
Merely Talking   131
The Worth in Looking Up   132
Fringe   133
Time Reborn   134
Eye Do   135
Alone   135
Much ado about nothing   135
Unknown Unseen   136
Big Thoughts, Little Ponders   137
What's the Use?   137
Protocol   138
Nature Calling   139
Something to Blow Your Mind   140
Rhapsody Arboreal   141
So What's Becoming   142
Written in Oblivion   143
Man of Wit   144
Upstart   144
Telling Tall Tales   145
Fester Benders   146
Whittle Awhile Away   147
A Path Once Taken   148
Demise of Conversation   150
Just words   151
Tomorrow's Gift   151
The Beginning   152

Chapter Fourteen:
Envisioning the Future

PREFACE

Just this morning, my thoughts returned to yesteryear;- to my youth and to my beginnings of exploring life and nature. What a better way to help me on my journey as a youth was to be a part of the Boy Scouts of America.

I began to recall all of the learning opportunities I had at my eager young fingertips. Countless disciplines were available for me to explore and learn; thus increasing and expanding my knowledge, - rounding out my outlook on life. What a wonderful way to get a sound start on my journey.

I worked my way up through the ranks from a Tenderfoot to an Eagle Scout, from a Patrol Leader to a Scoutmaster as an adult, from a learner to a Merit Badge Counselor, from a camper to a camp staffer to a Waterfront Director. All of that time, exploring and learning; then teaching and learning all over again. The process of scouting was so broad scope in its concept; that today, upon reflection, my mind is still boggled with all that I accumulated in those early years.

Without any aforethought; allow me to reminisce with you and reiterate all the areas of study that I ventured into with a gusto and enthusiasm so enthralling. The methodology of learning was an achievement called a merit badge. Some merit badges were required to advance through the ranks, from Tenderfoot to the Eagle Scout level. A scout could achieve further heights by meriting in groups of five; to further gain Bronze, Silver or Gold Palms. He could go even further by doubling or tripling the palms if he had time in the learning span of six years(twelve through eighteen years of age).

Merit badges consisted of more than one hundred thirty or more areas of study. The rise to Eagle required that you achieve twenty one designated badges. Not in any particular order they were as follows: Lifesaving, Swimming, First Aid, Personal Health, Public Health, Safety, Camping, Cooking, Civics, Nature, Bird Study, Conservation, Forestry, Pioneering, a choice of either Athletics or Personal Fitness, and six elective badges of your choice. I chose Astronomy, Archery, Home Repairs, Architecture, Art. and Mechanical Drafting. I went on to acquire six additional badges; - Pathfinding, Hiking, Chemistry, Canoeing, Rowing and Leathercraft. In retrospect, the learning scope was so vast and comprehensive, one could only marvel at the extant to which one could diversify and expand his knowledge.

Times change, and through the years, interests and technologies evolved into to areas of study. Merit badge categories changed as well. Civics changed to Citizenship (in three separate and required badges: - To the Community, To the Nation, and To the World). Conservation merit badge became two required choices: - Ecology, and Environmental Studies. Aeronautics and Space Exploration were added to the list. Of course, badges such as Botany, Biology, Geology, Animal Husbandry, Agriculture, Farming, Metalworking, Woodworking, Horsemanship, Dairy Husbandry, Basketry, Rifle, Fishing, Engineering and many, many others, both old and new are still around.

What a tremendous opportunity for a youth to be able to expand his mind library beyond his scholastic achievements. I am glad I had the chance. The early experience was the first of many learning discoveries that molded my direction and aided me in reaching for my vision.

Forever learning, I envision myself reaching for that goal in life. At any age, the future always looks bright. I anticipate and welcome the continuing journey.

Breathe

On a crag with Him by my side
Where majestic wonders do abide
Taking in our horizon's breadth
Wistful dreams – sustained breath

I ask Him how all this came to be
How were you able to create a tree
Or all the things of earth and sky
I ask you Lord: How? And why?

He looked at me for quite a while
Then offered me a heartfelt smile
And quietly whispered in my ear
Relax-inhale-breathe-hark- and hear

All that I've dreamt is my master plan
Molded thru love and my faith in man
Everything evolved from a single cell
Nature took over and nurtured it well

You, my soul steward, accepted earth
Destined to value your life from birth
To that day when you come unto me
With a grateful love received so free

Lord, that's a burden I strive to bear
I am relaxed, inhaling and I do care
I breathe, bringing in every thought
For I heed what you have wrought

Hiawatha's Hiatus

Sense the rhythm of the river
As the hush begins to quiver
While silver slivers slither by
Listen to its whispering sigh
Tone on tone forever poignant
Flowers flowing oh so buoyant
Swirling dreams inducing spell
Eddies spin where spirits dwell

The Garden of Vegan

    Let us stop here and pause for just a moment.
    Hark! Shush! Listen!
    An enchanting hush emanates from the edge of the verdant forest. A vibrant living labyrinthine oasis spreads out before you. Staring into its depths, the mystery of the darkness is disturbingly overwhelming, yet intriguingly inviting.
    Without warning, your intellect is challenged as you are being thrust into an adventurous game. For now you are being charged to search this denizen for runes or enigmas imbedded within. From the very outset of this verbal outpouring; essences of edible vegan herbs, veggies, and other produce have been cleverly seeded into the forest textured venue.

        Heed to every scene and scheme
        Focus and discern every clue
        Hark unto all sounds that teem
        You are alone in your own milieu
When you have reached the end, I've alerted

U. R. the Detective, to provide the answers. No way will I be able to enable you. Take your time. Now! Go seek and you shall find!

Your initial footfall as you venture into the forest is quite startling; - a sage old great horned owl gives a hoot. His presence brings peace within and you are comfortably set at ease. You stand in total awe as you eye a wren's wee nest with a solitary egg planted in it's cozy twig bottom. Gazing upward through the bay leaf canopy, the peeping blue-perfect sky is peppered with curious clumps of cotton. At your feet, amidst the ferns, silky mushrooms emit mini-karat dewdrop sparkles as the emerging day unfolds its splendor. If today were Tuesday and you were in Belgium; you might even espy some succulent Brussels sprouting. But, too bad, you are not in Belgium.

As ecstatic as it is, you sense that some impish trouble is about to occur. And sure enough, a gnome with a pipe in his mouth and a teeny beanie on his noggin; is having a rhubarb with you because you stepped upon and completely squashed his prize truffles! *"Once: You are a cabbage-head! Twice: You are a rapscallion, and Thrice: You are a dimwitted doodle-noodle nincompoop!"*, he cackles and chides vehemently.

Then, after scrambling and stumbling in confusion, you strike another blunder blow. Three faerie sisters,- Rosemary, Ginger, and Sella Ree screech bloody murder as you take a nervous leek all over their parsley-potato patch! Even the stag horn sumac turns beet-red over this bumbling, stumbling, embarrassing predicament. Now you are really in a pickle. Not even the bulging cornucopia of rutabaga, asparagus, cauliflower, rampion, and broccoli can save you now.

You dart through the forest furrows seeking shelter from your delirium. You happen upon the tree of knowledge. What!! Grabbing the forbidden tomato, you devour it.

Storming out of the forest's din with spin aching chagrin; you accidently end up sporting a case of the contagious slick chic-hives. Frantically, you try a cucumber and flax salve, then a dill and onion poultice, and finally a mace and watercress ointment. Nothing works. This itch is a bitch! *"Goodbye cruel world"* you scream to no one in particular. Alas! Even Mother Nature pays you no mind. And the hallowed forest returns to the solace of shadowed silence.

If you found forty one items lurking, you almost mastered the task; for there really are forty four. Whew! Are we through?

Turn up the volume. Okrah's on TV.

Rhyme Surfing

Here I go again. When poetry ceases, I inevitably thrash for a bit; then scramble my brain and jot down anything that comes to mind. In most instances, poems or thoughts will be generated from the list.

Critical path
Landfall
Dude ranch
On a rift
Get the drift'
Haughty naughty
Moon halo
Someday
Flip the plan
Stuck up
When the cows come home
Flutter
Flip side
Wannabes
Redundancy

Most likely, I would leave them sit for a bit; and, upon returning; I would begin to write once again.

Now, having thought about this exercise; and reminiscing about my career as an architect; I recall doing the very same thing. When given a new project design challenge, I would leave the building and go to a movie or some other diversion; and later return to the task. My mind was fresh and eager to enter into defining the issues and moving towards solving the problem. Jigsaw puzzles, crosswords. mind benders; – they all are methodically treated similarly. Okay, I'm leaving now. You just sit. I'll see you in a bit.

Flutter

Seized by the lure of the unknowns unfolding
And insatiable thirst for any truths beholding
Instant emotions and new notions I'm thinking
When a flutter flitters by with lazy eyes blinking

Ancients told legends of men doing things
By fluttering creative wax feathered wings
To venture skyward where an angel sings
Striving in vain to pluck the sun's strings

Nature portrays a similar mysterious sight
Of a moth so enticed in the still of the night
To flitter and flutter on its intriguing flight
As it turrets upward to the moon so bright

An alluring siren flutters her seductive eyes
As she shimmers, exposing voluptuous thighs
Our shuddering lips sputtering muttering cries
While stammering and stuttering decadent sighs

Augmenting Angst

In the forest deep; seeing no trees
No leaves abound – no sky – no breeze
All in queue for the eastbound el
Lost the token – scatterbrained hell
Flitter, flutter, flying belfry bats
Critters biting, – damn, it's gnats
    (everything is coming together -
        everything is falling apart)
Nervous pacing in the wings
Waiting 'til the fat lady sings
Standing where the buffalo roam
Waiting 'til the cows come home
Moonshine's fading into green
Seeing nothing ne'er being seen
    (a room full of strewn straws –
        grasping one - empty handed
    found my own file drawer
        a drawer of endless empty folders)
Shuffling papers – out of sorts
Seeking no one – mind aborts
Finally, finally getting the drift
Waking up in the graveyard shift
Muddling thru clipped clichés
Swift emergencies from the daze
    (all the puzzle pieces fit –
        yet the puzzle has no pictures
    time slides as Dali melts
        head splits as Picasso fractures)

Where on God's earth are we now?
Toiling, tilling behind a paper plow
Toiling , tilling 'til the ends of time
Rehearsed – waiting for the rhyme
Dreams – as a star – are far out there
I'm now a wretched wreck somewhere
      (in a frantic race of rats – spied my own tail out front
         took over the commanding lead
         in a Shakespearian tragedy
    received a healthy reality check
        damn thing bounced)
Somewhere down the dratted drain
Holding together against this strain
Butterflies scream – fluttering astray
Catching my breath ere it flies away
Mine eyes are dim – I cannot see
Oh good god – an urge - must pee
    (Act One. Scene One. Action.)
Curtain's up! Audience grins.
And my opening line begins.
    (on cue – I break a leg – I nailed it.)
Applause; - applause
Bravo; - cheer
Stand up; - stand up
Raves endear
Over; - over
Relief is here.
Now is the time.
Go grab a beer!

Flow

    To wander thru a meadow flow
    With tassels swaying to and fro
    To lift adrift with pillows soft
    Releasing all my cares aloft
    To sit beside a flowing stream
    Where tho'ts begin and ideas dream
    To allow a word as 'flow' move you
    When whims afford another view
    From where no other soul has trod
    To the caring hands of a loving God
    A burning, yearning reach to crave
    To this end I flow and enter brave

Circles

"What goes around; comes around."
    Dogs chasing their own tails
    Wishing wells and water pails
    Holding hands around a campfire
    A full moon or our shining sun
    Lunar, solar and angel halos
    Raindrop falling on a still pond
    A symbol of unity; or of oneness
    Dancing around a Maypole
    Rings on fingers and donut holes
    Orbits of almost any kind
    Wheels, wheels, - big and small
    Merry-go-rounds and hula hoops
    Cycles of life and circus rings
    Circle 'round the pleasant things
"Round and round she goes.
Where she stops, no one knows"

The Dunce in the Corner

Red conical cap
On his noggin
Comical fool
Sittin' on a stool
Corner lurkin'
Silent urchin
Get the picture?
What's he thinkin'?

I'm just sitting here
Back in the corner again
Living the life of a dunce
She got my dander up
By calling me a nerd
I called her a turd
She stuck her tongue out, so I whacked her

She says she hates me
She hates my guts. She's nuts.
But I really think she likes me
She likes to get me into trouble
I like to burst her prissy bubble
She stuck her tongue out, so I whacked her

Known as the mean one
"Look out for him", she says
I am not being mean
I'm the one with all the 'A's
She's just jealous
She stuck her tongue out, so I whacked her

I don't mind being in the corner
I have time to think a lot
I have time to dream a lot
I even plan how to get her goat
Then she will whine and tattle
And we will wail and battle
She will stick her tongue out;
          by then I will have whacked her

To be dunce is pretty cool
I hear all the lessons
I don't have to raise my hand
I don't have to speak
My turf corner is my land
I can't see her
I feel her tongue's stuck out;
          so mentally I whacked her

I've grown accustomed to this spot
Though aloof and antisocial I am not
Now I can say that, at least, for once
I don't mind having been the dunce
As for all that prissy feline chatter
Her antics no longer seem to matter
Comfort's given by my caring hand

Omens Imaged

As specters slink thru shades and shadows
Lonely thoughts drone these wiles of man
As the strident calling of befalling waters
Spins rasping rivers teasing shifting sand

Take from thee the love of cherished warriors
Who once graced thrones of castles torn
Let us not be burdened by the troubles carried
Nor be a hindrance to any imagery borne

As I stroll along the winding paths of glory
And thru the majestic glades of a sylvan fen
Let me relate an old never ending story
About who stood then and came from when

These were creatures who had yet to waken
No language learned; no thoughts foreseen
Destined deeds were lone gone – forsaken
Spineless sleaze - squandered - mean

Words were spoken yet never heard
Silent ideas lost in saddened sound
Thoughts were heard yet not spoken
Images were sought yet never found

Born to die without ever living
Born to salve their battle scars
Born to live a life unforgiving
Born to dwell beyond the stars

(continues)

To travel on thru endless times
To love conflict so cherished dear
To stand true to spiteful climes
To rend souls while shunning fear

Their purpose to live perhaps in doubt
What could life give these alien souls?
Their purpose to siege and strut about
As beings portraying ghoulish roles

Creation stirred as dawn did break
What was seen wasn't what was sought
While observing turmoil in its wake
Omens imaged left whims distraught

The day was ordained to cease – to end
Gasping in a torrent of anguished pain
A time to heal   -   and a time to mend
A time to start all over and to try again

Idle Hours

> Idle hours - pampered flowers
> Awaken before emerging dawn
> Greater loves are borne this day
> Persistent woes - forever gone
>
> Cricket calling - keen eyes befalling
> Regal swan gliding from the gloom
> Heartfelt thoughts of cherished love
> Gather bonding in the loving room

Move and Shake

Nothing left in my thinking grid
Not a word from the voice of id
Not well versed am I right now
Got to get going now somehow

Another day to wake and wonder
Another day to praise and ponder
To think a moment or two longer
Good rhymes may grow ever stronger

Softly Falls the Light of Day

Quickly snuff the candle wick
Morning light comes oh so quick
Bright ideas have turned me on
All before the welcomed dawn

Could there be another way?
Could I sculpt a bust of clay?
Could thoughts unshackled be?
Could my actions set me free?

Allegro tempo – run the race
Swiftly, swiftly - hasten pace
Don't stop now – night is nigh
No time to stop or wonder why

Get it done before the morrow
Reap the joy; forget the sorrow
Seize the day of wondrous light
Gain all you can before the night   (continues)

Softly falls the light of day
As our firelight fades away
Silently each of us should ask
Have we done our daily task?

As we've wandered o'er this land
Have we offered a helping hand?
Go forth the night and hold it dear
May our dreams be crisp and clear

The Start of Something Big

Something was astir;
Something was coming
The wild was calling
The Oracle of the Ark was nigh
And they came out in vast hordes
From everywhere to be with everything
From the jungle – the mighty jungle
From the sea – the bounding sea
From the sky – the clouds up high
From the mountain - from the lea
From the caves - from the forest
From the rivers - from the tree
Everything came – just everything
An alphabetical alliteration from A to Z

Aardvark, aster, auk, ant, amoeba, and antelope came
Bear, beetle, bee, begonia, boa, bat, birch, and butterfly
Cacti, cat, crocus, cougar, cantaloupe, clam, and cricket
Dandelion, deer, dolphin, dog, and dormouse came
Eagle, eel, elephant, elk, emu, elm, eft and eucalyptus

Falcon, fly, flea, flounder, the frog and the flycatcher
Giraffe, gorilla, guava, gull, gator, gnat, and grouse
Halibut, horse, hamster, hare, holly, and the hippo
Ibex, ibis, impatiens, indigo bunting, and even the ivy
Jackal, jaguar, jasmine, jay, and jack-in-the-pulpit came
Kangaroo, koala, kiwi, kookaburra, kinkajou, kumquat
Lacewing, ladybug, lamb, lark, larkspur, leopard, lynx
Macaw, marmoset, monkey, mushroom, moose, myrtle
Nautilus, nuthatch, nutmeg, and the nighthawk came
Ocelot, octopus, olive, orchid, oriole, otter, onion, owl
Pansy, panda, papaya, partridge, pear, phlox, penguin
Quince, quail, quahog, and even the Queen Ann's lace
Raccoon, radish, rail, ray, robin, rhino, raven, rooster
Sassafras, shark, seal, serpent, skink, skunk, and swan
Tadpole, thistle, tarantula, tiger, toad, and turtle came
Umbrella tree, unicorn, and even the upland plover
Venus's flytrap, vetch, vole, violet, vireo, and vulture
Walking stick, wallaby, walrus, wasp, whale, weevil
Xanadu - the gathering spot
Yak, yam, yarrow, yellowtail, yew, and yucca came
Zebra, zebu, zinnia, and the zucchini

They all came to Xanadu – an idyllic, beautiful place
The Kingdom of Heaven on Earth
All living things came, - except for Man
For an earthly crisis was of utmost concern
For it was now that the Nature of God proclaimed:
> *All living things present are hereby alerted;*
> *For the Wrath of God would strike Man down*
> *For Man:*
>> *Has desecrated the face of the Earth*
>> *Has held no regard for the welfare*

>   *Or the health of the planet*
>   *Has not fulfilled his stewardship in*
>   *Protecting one and all*
>   *Including his own kind*
>   *Has denigrated the cycle of life*
>   *Has taken complete domination*
>   *Over everything on Earth*
>   *Uncaring for other forms of Life*
> *We, the flora and fauna of this, our Earth,*
> *From this day forward:*
>   *Do duly recognize our responsibilities*
>   *Do hereby take sole occupancy*
>   *Do henceforth steward, maintain, nurture,*
>   *And enhance Life for All*
>   *Becoming One with Nature and God*

Mankind will stand subservient to our commands.
We will survive
We will thrive!
Save the planet
Long live the Earth.
And the sky cried
The sea sighed
Swelled
And rolled over
Swallowing the land
And silence came onto the Earth

Alma Mater Avalanche
Cascading Chaos
Campus Calamity
Hell Week
November Nightmare
Fallen Feelings
Secrets Hiding Lies
Please Pass the Hope

Any title will do
At good ole' PSU
No soul had a clue

A darkened cloud
A secret shroud
O'er the campus flew

Pillars standing tall
Pillars fail and fall
Untruths begin to brew

Images maintained
Pedestals retained
Happy Valley turning blue

Every emotion is relevant
Every child is heaven sent
Pure as life thru and thru

Begin the healing
Love that feeling
Hope is nigh for me and you

Where am I going?

Is this what destiny is all about?
Duck the shot
Feel the luck
Purge the urge
Now's the time to rise and shout
Taken by a sun-drenched stream
To the inner sanctum of a dream
A rambling mind is put to task
To seek and find a happy mask
> *In the swells trout are flowing*
> *In the caves worms are glowing*
> *In the meadow seeds are sowing*
> *In the knowing all is growing*

The path ahead appears enigmatic
Each footfall taken warily ecstatic
Thoughts no longer lay in my hand
Poetic muse lost in some never land

Unfound   In the middle of a haystack
In an old abandon barn surround
Hiding from persistent seekers
A steely eye stood its ground
Nothing moved; prevailing silence
What is hidden may ne'er be found
The eye of steel; eluding madness
Digs deftly into shards profound
Feats of glory passing tests of time
Warm hearts felt by souls abound
Many a story leaves feelings empty
Needle pulled a coup; - hands down

Just three little words

    A college architectural design assignment was handed to everyone in the class. The given problem was to design a railroad station which handled pedestrians, auto and bus traffic, parking, as well as train arrivals and departures. The site, situated in a Pittsburgh urban environment, was restricted and irregular in shape. Alcoa Aluminum Corporation was the sponsor and bequeathed cash prizes for the best designs. The final concept had to incorporate the use of aluminum in both practical and innovative implementations.

    My design came to me relatively swiftly and I was pleased with my result. The circulation of all modes of movement by people, bus and auto traffic flow, parking, baggage handling, ticketing, waiting, and the boarding and departing of passengers was working beautifully. I used the application of aluminum in many ways and I developed a sculptured aluminum panel that became the exterior skin for my design of the railroad station.

    Great! But something wasn't working. The building footprint did not function well on the site. My Professor/Design Advisor was making his routine critiquing rounds to all of his students. He arrived at my table and I showed him my conceptual sketches and drawings. I talked of how the flow of all disciplines moved effectively and efficiently; but expressed my frustration with the flow of traffic on the site. He looked pleased, smiled and said just three little words; *"Flip the plan."* And then he walked away. (continues)

I just stood there perplexed. Peering down at the design, I suddenly saw how the flip would solve my dilemma. Leaving the site design intact; I flipped the building footprint and everything fell into place perfectly.

Several weeks later, presentations were made by each design contestant to Alcoa reps and faculty judges. The reviewing team conferred and then the award ceremony took place. I walked away with the best design and the top award. My fellow students told me afterwards that they knew that I had the best solution – hands down! What a tremendous feeling.

To this very day, now sixty six years later and still counting, I have never forgotten those three most important little words; *"Flip the plan."*

The lesson told me to always "think outside of the box." You can never go wrong.

The Horizontal Lab

Many of my friends and acquaintances ask me; *"When do you write all the poems? How do you generate your poems?"* I always respond with; *"When I am in my horizontal lab."*

My horizontal lab is that sleep/wake, dream state, dawn break, slip-sliding, in and out, ideas developing, word shaping, in bed and oh-so-cozy time of day. Sometimes the entire poem is a dream. But most times a thought, a catch phrase, or a single word becomes the catalyst for a poem's birth. A pre-breakfast scamper to the computer and a quick jot-down of the thought is all I need. The best poems are the easiest to write for they flow like quicksilver from my thought processor to my fingertips.

When I was a kid, oft times, day dreaming and wondering –
if I could – what would I 'wannabe'?
Wannabes
I wannabe a manatee, fat and blubbery
        Wallowing and bobbing
        In the warm clear blue spring
        All day and every day
        Glub – glub bubbly
        Nah, not for me
I wannabe a wallaby, big hind feet below me
        Bouncing around the outback
        With a baby in the belly sac
        All day long
        A bobbing bouncing joey
        Nah, not for me
I wannabe a chimpanzee, high in a jungle tree
        Swinging and flying
        Picking bugs off one another
        Yuk – all day long – double yuk
        Bug off monkey
        Nah, not for me
I wannabe a bumblebee, so busy being busy
        Into buzzing flowers
        Pollen nectar, nectar bowers
        All day long
        Buzz off busy bee
        Nah, not for me
I wannabe a chickadee in cozy nest in a tree
        Singing, tweeting
        Flying, fleeting
        Hmmm; that would be neat
        Toodle-ooo, tweedle-dee
        But (sigh), I guess not for me   (cont)

I wannabe a Jim dandy; - footloose and fancy free
        Wallowing, bouncing, bobbing
        Singing, swinging, tweeting
        Maybe even flying, fleeting
        Doing different things
        All day and every day
        So dandy, so happy, so free
        Yep, that's for me

Transformers

Barely survivable
Crawling redundancy
In a torn misguided world

Shunned by society
Seeking accountability
In this cozy cocoon curled

Sustained comfort
Anticipating hopefully
While being snugly squirreled

Newfound enlightenment
Emerging energetically
With exploding wings unfurled

Together So near and yet so far away
Posed a still-life lovely face
Seeing you standing lonely
In a flowering field of clover
In some imagined alien land
Yearning arms outstretched
Stepping through the frame
I saw us both no longer lonely
In the field of imagined clover
Standing there hand in hand
Therein we stayed forever
In our imagined friendly way
We saw happiness for us only
In this field of fragrant clover
Far away but yet oh so grand

Reign Refrain Bursts of wrath
Slashing strife
Hurling drops
Controlling life
Thru time and time again
Perched on the leading edge
Overburdened
Grieving
Releasing
Falling into oblivion
Falling, falling forever
Unless caught in life's cistern
In the abyss of time
Now no longer subservient
Never to reign again

Stuck Up

Whether history
Or family; or lists
Or tasks done daily
The home file story
In whole life glory
Stuck up
On the fridge
Stuck up reminders
A convenient Motherboard
Dogs and cats and magnet ads
Kids and Moms and even Dads
Haphazardly arranged
Nothing pompous
Nothing contrived
A memory smorgasbord
Just stuff
Lots of stuff
Stuck up

Moon Halo

        Reverent bearing
        Full moon wearing
        Mystique flaring
        Oh! The halo of crystal light
Silence staring
Brilliance glaring
Seduction sharing
    Oh! The miracles so bright
Intrigue uprooting
Sage owl hooting
Silence rebooting
Oh! The wisdom of the night

All that happened wasn't meant to be.
Clan – destiny

Secretly, silently
Purloined passion
Fractured frenzy
Lust in drag
Exhumed from a vulture
Born of a culture
Far beyond dreams perceived
Mindless followers
Sheep of faith; - taken
Torn fleece of dread
Broken instead
Shards of doubt
Strewn about
Corrupted creeds
Deeds of malicious seeds
Kept in contempt
Never exempt
Imprisoned in shadows
Black dawn looming
In utter misery
Blooming dead
Wisdom may rise
Opening eyes
To skies without lies
Believe; yea, believe
Receive
Letters of intent
Meant
For their very own true destiny

The macrocosm of life is merely an overview;
a summary of everything found in the embodiment
of all things ever believed.

Sometimes in Rhyme

Thoughts spoken
Thoughts written
    Yesterday
    Today
    At work, at play
All weave a pattern
    Of life molded
    Or remolded
        In mime
Sometimes in rhyme
Teasing thoughts
    Spontaneous
    On purpose
    Unconscious
All jotted down
Threads intra-woven
    Momentarily
    Stitched in time
Sometimes in rhyme
Appearing haphazardly
    As raindrops fly
    Seemingly from
    An empty sky
Appearing as a tiny tale
        Told in time
Sometimes in rhyme

            (continues)

Thoughts plucked
> From life's thesaurus
> From life's dreams

Miracles return
> From wherever
> Whenever
> Any old time

Sometimes in rhyme

And the vignettes of life go on
> and on
> > and on.

Dream Building Team

Today stood four muted prospectors
Sculptor, musician, designer, director
Separate in their individual dreams
Eight hands held palette and brush
Four mind-sets held to silence – hush
Before them stood a stark white scene
With palette and apron and attitude
Approaching the task with fortitude
Strokes of color turned canvas alive
Blades of grass in a flora frenzy drive
A mauling jungle morass did thrive
Dark, foreboding spooky hocus-pocus
The sylvan mayhem loomed – no focus
Until the dawning brought the light
Sunbeams splashing through the night
Bringing promises of a life so bright
> (continues)

A beginning came to seed and to feed
Designed as with music, filled the air
Sculpted and artistically directed there
A floating, blooming mushroom grew
Energy bursting; hope blossoming anew
All enraptured by a flock - clad crew
Mission accomplished; they all knew
As the four stood there proudly as one
Foundation laid – a dream had begun
Yet that very day stood two other teams
Happy relief bursting at all their seams
As now the moment dawned unto each
Together there's a mission for us to reach

Tirades on a Rampage

Angry mobs with hateful zombie eyes screaming
Spume wild thoughts from oral chasms of despair
Hell-bent to desecrate good cringing in the wings
Shock-poets writing scared in evil spirited rhyme
Not solving, yet soiling already disturbed minds
Ghouls trample troubled souls into bloodied sheep
Salivating festered glands with fang-dripped meat
Relent! Gargoyles rant and cry. Relent, admit defeat!

Why, oh why?
There are flutter byes. There are busy bees
There is a lovely forest through these trees
Is there any person out there who disagrees?
Is there any person out there who truly sees?
As I beg you now from these humble knees
Tell me this very moment sir; - if you please
                                    (continues)

This poet seeks and sees the beauty everywhere
In mind, in spirit and everything here and there
Anticipating daily miracles; in humble awe, I stand
Excited with all earth's natural wonders planned
Thrilled that my eyes bear witness to all the beauty
What happens around me becomes my precious duty
To not only save but savor in a most protective way
All life and love providing comfort every single day

This poet will not relent to these psycho fiends
Those who regurgitate repugnant festering weeds
Do not bury your fear with satisfying grins
Do not laud the tsunami of anti-healing spins
No longer may the denizens of dark rule the land
Right here there is much to see and to understand
Deter nonsense; stop the grief. Open doors; seek relief
Fight like warriors; defend your life; hold to your belief

One could go on but what's the point?
Our funny bone is already out of joint
Strong feelings have now been spent
Nowhere else to turn; nor else to vent
When goodness prevails; there's no fear
Take leave with kindness cherished dear

Nightlight
night on night
darkness seeking darkness
never waking
never sleeping, never dreaming
darkness chasing darkness
lightness chasing darkness
lightness cleansing darkness
sleeping
dreaming, waking
lightness seeking lightness
light on light

> *"Your future is created by you, for you;*
> *built from your own dreams,"*
> T. Goodkind: <u>The Omen Machine</u>

End Times
until
prophesies
send falling skies
into eclipsing epochs
where omens impend
where signs portend
counting days
time stands still
and the dead sense time
as an illusion
so time ends
non-dimensionally
unbounded
time comes again
those living sense time
as a reality
until

Until

Purple, deep purple skies
Vivid, violent, violating
Vindictive vandals' cries
Van Gogh painted visages
Falling as frogs, as locusts
Looming thru the gloom
Masticating doom
Spun on a spider's loom

Until serenity stands
In glorifying hands
Demands; yea commands
For all doubts to release
Vile and raging; all do cease
Vow! To stay all troubles now!
Worries wept and withered
Sorrows sulked and slithered

Until daytime comes and rises
And morning dew surprises
As the cleansing firmament
Brings needed nourishment
To freshen hearts; uplifting spirits
To awaken souls; renewing births
Understated and unrehearsed
Life is good for me and you

Until that day, come walk with me
Love me as I love you
Love me beyond all dawns and dreams
Until forever comes to be – for me and you

Here is an exercise. put into rhyme, exploring random thoughts which just might end up in a poem.

Couplet Capers

Oh so sleepy
Dream's so creepy
    Being naughty
    Feeling haughty
Plod along
Sing a song
    Taking chances
    Stealing glances
Hidden treasures
Buried pleasures
    Windshield wipers
    Scotland pipers
Toes are tapping
Pebbles dapping
    Snow's a-drifting
    Spirits lifting
Fingers snapping
One hand clapping
    Joys for boys
    Tinker toys
Golden swirls
Curls for girls
    Dream shapers
    Couplet capers

Scrapbook Snapshots

Born
First light, so bright
Bubbling, bouncing baby boy
Naturally naïve, unknowing
Yet glowing, learning, growing

Tots
Toys, more toys and sister's tricks
Games of catch and pick up sticks
Tethered to a pole when naughty
Winning games made me haughty
Erector sets and Lincoln Logs
Teddy bears and puppy dogs

Teens
Switching gears
During awkward years
Acne fears
Restraining tears

Scouting
Camping, cooking, swimming, hiking
Everything in nature to my liking
Advancing to the rank of Eagle
Enduring exploration in a life so regal

In-betweens
Those times before
Turning twenty one
Biding time
Enjoying the fun   (continues)

Solitude
Getaway places
Secluded spaces
Heaven's graces
In my embraces

Social Life
Parties, parties
Seeing faces, breaking breads
Parties, parties
Heavy hearts, groaning heads

Jersey Shore
Summer soirees at the shore
Suntanned bodies, eyes are sore
Nighttime parties and much more
Each day better than the day before

Nittany Lion
College life chasing dreams
On your own, learning themes
Life is built with plots and schemes
Enjoyment bursting at the seams

Graduation
Granted an Architectural degree
Feeling foot loose and fancy free
Celebrating with pomp and fling
Swam in dam – lost college ring

(continues

Wedding Day
Double bride, double grooms
Double kisses, two less misses
Double gowns with double cakes
A day to remember this day makes

Puerto Rico and Manhattan
United States Navy boot camp drills
New experiences, new learned skills
Two different duties, four years of life
One alone, three with my lovely wife

Busyness
Decades of designed intentions
Awards, innovations, inventions
Totally loving every minute
There is no other way to spin it

Vacations
Caribbean isles, Madrid, Majorca
Italy Monaco, Nice and Cannes
Casino Royale and Le Mans
Cuba, Chichen Itza and Tulum
San Juan, Caneel Bay and Cancun
Little Dix, the Baths in Virgin Gorda
Big Sur, Montreal and Quebec City
Thousand Islands and Cape Cod
Woodstock Inn and both Disney's
From Key West to Bar Harbor
From Tijuana to Muir Woods
Through thirty states, scads of cities
All the while, writing ditties

                                  (continues)

Sons
Four we shared
Watched them grow
From boys to men
And then some

Sports
Player, watcher, give, or taker
Tennis , golf, and volleyball
Quoits, horseshoes, croquet troublemaker
Skiing, college football in the fall

Grandsons
Josh and Adam
Blue eyed boys
Lots of hugs and kisses
For me and my missus

Fiftieth Wedding Celebration
Munich in heavenly May
Train trip to an alpine top
Sound of music in the air
Salzburg fling, hearts so fair

Poetry
With strengthened heart
Forever seeking, baring soul
Sixty years of writing rhyme
My life journey; well worth the time

(continues)

Retirement
A time to reminisce
A time not to miss
A time to review
A time to renew
Never intending to drift
Down South so far
To Florida we flew
To a Haven so Grand
To a paradise land
New fun we found
New friends abound
Never thought
It would come to this
Enchantingly bliss
Sealed with a kiss

End of the Trail
My cottage in the wood
In solitude so I stood
And if I ever could
Forever I forever would

Emotional Game   One day a little bird of blue
While perching on a spade
Off the handle flew
Winged it and withdrew
Tweeted the house
Split the deck down the middle
Ran the table up a cloudy draw
Not in the cards; not a big deal
Shoulder-blocked his chips; - and flew the coup

Life's roadmap of pleasurable times meanders on.
Joyous thoughts inevitably encounter road bumps
      while traveling on its merry learning journey.
For no explainable or reasonable basis; sad thoughts do
      pop up; then happily and abruptly disappear.
Just as it did right here!

Lonely Hearts Club

As I stepped aside and wiped away a tear
I heaved a sigh and exclaimed, "Oh, dear."

What is in my heart no longer lingers there
No whims dare part nor do thoughts declare

All that is left within self is left within soul
Forever torn apart within my body whole

What's done is done; nothing else to fear
All that is gone now, will never reappear

A golden heart continues its will to survive
Thanks be to God that I am still quite alive

A craving to live overriding a craving to die
As I stepped aside no longer wondering why

Nit-picking Nonsense

No heresy, lore, or even a fable
About how Cain disabled Abel
For with a cane I am quite able
To be direct – remaining stable

Conversing with One's Self

During the dews of early morning rises
Spurred by spirits of wondrous might
Are you aware of what's around you?
Can you see and appreciate the light?

You, with a nagging nuance gnawing
In the bosom of your overburdened heart
Dare your soul echo a solemn silence?
Or allow spirits to stoically stand apart?

So this morn, enjoy the present moment
Be aware of gifts given lovingly to you
Let your hopes and dreams emerge
Enjoy today refreshed – alive – anew

Another day to play
Another foray to go astray
Scramble

Sitting somewhere in a hazy daze
      Solving this puzzle; everything's coming apart
      Have I the answer; or am I the puzzle?
Am I a maze within a maze?
      Seeing myself as a blur
      Phasing in and out
      Appearing here and there
      Wandering about
      Mired in doubt
      Nearing everywhere
      Yet being nowhere
      In a tizzy; oh so dizzy
Am I an abyss?
      Beyond the edge of this cliff of bliss
      Nothing's in place
      Even the dreams are in a briar bramble
      What's left to gamble?
Am I like a peanut hiding under a shell?
      Playing games and tricks
      Fooling only myself
      Shedding lazy tears
      Dancing the Muskrat ramble?
As I scramble for a foothold
      My earth disappears; torn asunder
      Escaped to another wonder
To be or not; lest time forgot
Standing on faith so bold
      I teach myself to fly
            To soar to someplace high

Who let the cat out of the bag? Scat, but don't kill it!

Curiosity

Going there is one thing
Getting there is another
Staring blank
No ideas come; nothing clicks
The mind plays tricks
Shapes take form from the norm
As a curious mind delves
Frenzied fingers fervently rush
Eager words spell themselves
Across the once silent screen

> *Seek no more; you have found me*
> *My domain is now for the taking*
> *Sweet dreams are in the making*
> *You only have eight more to go*

Found who? Domain; whose domain?
Why me? Eight more what?

> *I am Felicia. My domain is yours.*
> *Your dreams are mine.*
> *I am yours to command.*
> *Now you have only seven.*

Felicia who? Seven more what?
Who are you to command what of me?
What the hell's going on?
                    (continues)

Hell is going on.
    Lives dummy, lives!
    Felicia Mew; here to
    Command your destiny.
    Now you have six.

The hell you say; I don't know any Felicia Mew.
Lives? Destiny? Nix to six! What did I do?

    Cat's got your tongue?
    You are still quite alive,
    Goodness, you're now down to five.

You must be kidding me.
Stop this freaking game!

    Can't stop this game;
    But yes, it's freaking.
    Something's in store.
    Don't open that door.
    You're now down to four.

Store!? Door!? Four!? I'm going berserk!
You are making me out to be a jerk.

    Whatever you say;
    Your destiny follows.
    No matter which way;
    Beware of the shallows.
    Now mercy me; You have only three.

(continues)

Damn it! This is absolutely asinine!
Every time I open my fat mouth;
This smartass cat knocks me shitless!
This is a catastrophe!
What the hell can I do? Oops, don't answer that.

> *Oh, too late. You already made a date.*
> *Now we must calmly sit and wait.*
> *No turning back; the door has shut*
> *Free yourself from the awesome rut.*
> *Guess what? You're almost through;*
> *Now you're clock is striking two.*

Two pooh! Now I'm pissed!
You got me into this!
There is only one of me left'
Why didn't you tell me what is going down?
I hate you! I'm not feeling well. I'm sick
You might as well take my life now.

> *No, that would be too easy.*
> *You are a pushover, - a pussy!*
> *You have the right; where's your fight?*
> *Don't lose sight.*
> *Hang around. Stand your ground.*
> *Remember who you are.*
> *Remember that you are not done.*
> *Unfortunately though; now it's one.*

       (continues)

My name is Felix; Felix the Cat.
I sit on a fence. At the moon; I howl.
I love who I am and I am strong.
Now I know where this went wrong.
With me you toyed and taunted
With me, my life, you flaunted.
I am Felix; the Cat.
You took advantage of a sorry wuss.
A down-in-the-dumps - scared-y puss.
Well, I've had enough of you.

I don't need you. I don't want you.
I could care less about you; you bitch.
Take those nine lives and bite me.
I am Felix; the Cat. The bag ass-meow!
Watch your back; I'm on the prowl.

> *I am Felicia Mew. You are hot; purring me on.*
> *Your lives were never spent;*
> *Just a ruse so you'd relent*
> *Come to me my feline hunk;*
> *Let me curl about your trunk.*
> *Let's put your tomcat in my cradle.*
> *Fill up my cup with your silver ladle.*

What a condescending, sniveling, lying bitch.
Don't patronize or solicit me; you ugly witch!
Good riddance! This door I am now closing.
Vowing to never, freaking ever, blog again.

Curiosity has taken a powder
The screen went blank; turning silent once again.
Leaving here is one thing
Getting away from here is another

The world, like a dictionary, has so many places to visit.
Visiting Cities

Curiosity
Been there previously
Done that frequently
Obesity
A place where one doesn't want to be
Where south of the border is hard to see
Adversity
An adventure of a different kind
Once you're there; what a find
Diversity
Can I do this or dare I do that
This place always has a welcome mat
University
If you go there and haven't learned it
Then you certainly haven't earned it
Propensity
Magnets tend to push or pull
Yearns fill your life; -that's no bull
Velocity
A place swiftly up 'n coming
Now quickly gone and going
Varsity
Jocks, socks, all sweat and tears
Bums you out but builds careers
Simplicity
A place where all patterns are drawn and cut
And fitted forms are made to cover your butt
            (continues)

Veracity
In all, gall is divided into three tracts
Guts, balls, and reckless abandon acts
Intensity
Once you are there, you are really in it
There's no other way for you to spin it
Synchronicity
Impromptu visits provide opportunities to combine
Happenstance and commonality will naturally align
Eccentricity
Oddly enough, a place where nuts dwell
And scurrying squirrels bury them well
Electricity
You'll be shocked if you go there in the dark
Make sure you catch the ever awesome spark
Luminosity
A place where the aura of hope opens your door
While bringing light into your heart forever more

Being Shy

Secluded by the wayside
               In the bye and bye
               Hidden fears sigh
Teardrops tossed aside
               Left to slowly dry

Coyness remains cowering
               Waves breaking free
               Breezes bending tree
Yearnings overpowering
               No longer burden me

Parting Ways
Sturdy, swarthy, wickedly wild
Walking so haughty, eerily riled
Pleading frightfully, littlest child
Taken innocence, wretched tears
Triumphantly evil, slobbered fears
Family in turmoil, in silent running
Justice sits helpless, apathy shunning
Evil prevails, shockingly stunning
Who counts their days?
Who mends their ways?
In parting, whose life strays?
Whose life remains .... **Adrift**
     I am a lone star
     A cosmic corsair
    Course not; time forgot
     Just drifting through
    I am a face in the crowd
     Bumping around
    Lone groupie in fugue
  Without purpose; without gain
     I am space dust
     List, lust-less
  Doing whatever, going wherever
      I am cork
     No longer popping
    Wave bopping, uncaring
    Not harried, just carried
     I am tumbleweed
   Sifting the sands of time
   Dreamless dune drifter
  Lifeless; just along for the ride
     (continues)

Whatever we do; wherever we go
Whoever we are
We need a purpose for being
A base for believing
A reason for seeing
A goal worth achieving

Carefree

Taken by the grains of sand
    Cavorting o'er the barren land
        Riding waves of soft sunbeams
            Sifting thoughts of secret dreams

Rising

Top of the morning to ole sol of might
    With your happy face so shiny bright
Hark to sound as a meadowlark sings
    Safe in the hands that dawning brings

Resemblance

Not of this world; strung out, hurled
      Connected strands, entwined hands
      Uniquely matched in common bands
      Everything is akin
      Created relativity, banned individuality
      Everything has been and will be again
      Images mirroring images
      Where green is green is green
      Before, behind, betwixt, between
Not on this world with life's coils curled
      Hands of time mired in muck
      Today is now forever struck
      Clay remolded into clay
      Sculptor's mind led astray
      Do as we do; see as we see
      Expressing redundancy
      Breaking brethren bread
      Woven from cloned thread
      Bramble bridges to nowhere
      Yet to everywhere
Not in this world; twirled but ne'er unfurled
      Where then is the wonder?
      The oneness of all; empathy of just being
      Togetherness by getting along
      Encircling life in rhyme and song
      Holding hands with all as written on the wall
      All was meant to be for everyone to see
      Preordained love; imagined, inbred
On this, our world, naturally knurled

Circa, either the seventies or the eighties, this event actually took place as presented. I was reading from the Afterword in an Omni Magazine to the gang who were at the party about the gofers and the frogs – and then it happened. Later, I wrote this poem and retold it to basically the same group. Lot's of fun.

Milligan's Lament

It was a warm summer's evening
Not one guest was leaving
Milligan's Gordon Street residence of yore

Eyes were all glowing
And beer kept on flowing
No one knew what the night held in store

I, with no hesitation
And no trepidation
told a tale that golfers will thoroughly abhor

I told of the Everglades
And the terrible escapades
Of tree frogs who dabbled in bloodlust and gore

A wayward shot careened from the tee
Flew into the woods and lay under a tree
"Help me to find it; without balls, I just cannot score"

From the woods, golfers came screaming
With eyes totally blank and tears screaming
Frogs on their heads, sucking their brains to the core
(continues)

All those hearing the sordid detailing
In disbelief, sat, all fearful and paling
What would com next. Tell us nothing; no more!

When suddenly on this sultry night
The damn-dist event put souls to flight
There's more to come; which you can't ignore.

Slippery, slimy slugs, sultans of sleaze
Fell from above; from the sycamore trees
Fell to our feet on this moss-laden brick patio floor

Shocked cries of dismay, disdain, and disgust
Echoed the night midst the raucous beer bust
Corky, the schnauzer, fled away like never before

This tale has been told and retold again
Not by women; but by only the men
May the frogs and slugs dare to soar nevermore

Redundancy

Hello – Hi – right here – so near
Alone – alone – afraid – I fear
I am really me and you are you
So long – bye-bye – ciao – adieu

In a Jaded Jungle

Wily critters cease their lowly creep
Lazing cats yawn as they try to sleep
Fleet of foot flop into a fluffy heap
Birds of feather tweet a lonely peep

Trees so still as they no longer sway
Silent minds with no games to play
Signs point us towards another way
Boredom breeds no thoughts today

Emerge scatterbrained twiddledums
Fingers mingling with their thumbs
Nothing is level; nothing plumbs
Yet blessings bring in tidy sums

Scissor – hands

Tales snipped
Quips clipped
Notes nipped
     Sheared sheep
     @#$%+& bleep
     Secrets keep
Minced meat
Kind of neat
Short, yet sweet

Star Struck
Stumbling thru darkened night
Winking stars shared insight
Heard them whisper oh so clearly
Loved that moment - oh so dearly
What they did was all important
Haunted hushes remain poignant
Tauntingly they teased my yearn
As a craven cavern yawns in turn
Lofted softly midst their grandeur
Spun thru time in blissful candor
No! This tryst dare not ever end
My wanton wallowing alien friend
Let them wander in their wonder
As drifting pillows cavort yonder
Stay here is this everlasting glen
Stars wink whimpers once again
Zephyrs unveil shrouded clouds
Sorrows seep from wily crowds
Summer smoke wafts and swirls
As a maven raven's curl unfurls
A wielding wand waving mourner
Emerges from a ghost – like corner
With eerie unearthly wails screeching
Demons within are forever preaching
What's been wrought by a thought
Nay! My soul can ne'er be bought!
Head up high – standing straight
I enter through a welcoming gate
No need to gasp or wonder why
Secrets scatter from a sparkling sky
Worlds spin thru darks and lights
Souls soar to even greater heights

Engaging Likeness

Out in the darkness
Secrets were hid
Madness within
Hunt will begin
Terror mind bender
Maniac personified
Man on a quest
To seek, to confront, to take down
Mythical Mastermind
Memys ElfandI
    A suicide mission
    To do or to die
    A task like no other
    Success must rely
    Thru cunning
    Thru stealth
    Thru surprise
    To seek, to confront, to take down
    Magical Mastermind
    Memys ElfandI
With keen tactics
With sharp mind
With quickness
Found and met
Face to face
Shattered image
In the mirror of time
Sought, confronted, taken down
Mystical Mastermind
Memys ElfandI

Just the other day, I heard an instrumental piece entitled:

How It Ends

How does it end?   How does what end?
What does "it" mean?   Is it life?
Or is it this world, our universe, me, you, this story, this
Poem, this year, this hour, this moment, this thought?
Do we really know?
Do we need to know how it does end, or even if it does?
Could I write a poem that has no end?   I did.
On July 30, 1987 I wrote:
>   *It is the beginning, not the end*
>   *A new start is just around the bend*
>   *And when I do go 'round next bend*
>   *It is the beginning, not the end*

And yet again, on July 31, 1992:
>   *Each new day brings a new dawn*
>   *Each new sunset sets anticipation for that new day*
>   *Each sleep seeks a new dream*
>   *Each raindrop comes from a new direction*
>   *Hits a new place... wets a new space*
>   *Each life brings a new life*
>   *Each new bud brings a new bloom*
>   *Each person met is a new friend found*
>   *Each of us is unique*
>   *We strive in parallel*
>   *Move congruently... live concurrently*
>   *We are peace... not turmoil*
>   *We are love...not hate*
>   *We are the beginning...not the end*
>   *...for there is no end*

Autumn Twilight

Turning leaves
Heartfelt heaves
A time to know
A time to grow
A time so old
Now foretold
Accustomed life
Assuming strife
Grinding gears
Wrinkled tears
Open minds
Life unwinds
Void cocoon
Smiling moon
Butterfly born
October morn

Have you heard?

Have you heard what could happen?
As a silly clown wears sodden frown
Wimps cavort with gigantic ogres
Something weird is coming down
An absurd nerd uttered not a word
While servile hosts in silence toiled
Hoots hollered in deepened hollows
Whispers crept while serpents coiled
Did you hear that hush grow ugly?
Scurrying frantic nymphs and gnomes
Fungi gleamed with envied essence
Toadstools danced midst catacombs
If one speaks, who then will listen?
If no one hears, then no one knows
Nonsense rules without any reason
That's just the way this poem goes

Of Pine Barrens

Standing so silent
Standing so tall
Straight as an arrow
Row upon row
Needles of pine
Softly sublime
Stalwartly
Stoic
Sentinels in time

Oath Renewal

I, James, take thee, Shirley, to be my. . .
    . . . to have and to hold . . .
    . . . from this day forward . . .
    . . . until death us do part . . .
All that I have to offer dear
I hold in my heart right here
These silent lips conceal
How strongly I really feel
   "I love you Shirley"
       - hidden – unspoken – unsaid
       - deep within – inside – instead
Well from this day forward; that must come to end
   From this day forward; I do this message send:
. . . I love you here . . . I love you now . . .
. . . I love you forever after . . .
. . . Here, now, and forever after . . .
. . . Death ne'er will us do part . . .
. . . I . . . Love . . . You . . . Shirley . . .

Genesis

Emerging annals of fabled lore
Spiriting delicious days of yore
Every thought must be favored
Every moment must be savored
Mysteries carved from creation
Wonders sculpted in adoration
Nebulae cluster in sense around
Secrets hide in a great surround

When writing anything down, though it may be uplifting; words begin at the top of the page, then continue downward toward some future intent. The reader with in- satiable enthusiasm, anticipates the outcome to be tantalizing; reads onward and downward.

Life goes on as a journey. When striving to reach a goal such as a mountain summit; the resultant view is a rewarding and dazzling accomplishment.

Imagine life's journey as a succession of larvae instinctively napping in cocoons and morphing into emerging butterflies; bursting into brave new worlds.

Souls in Motion

Free souls – cosmic dust – adrift
Sliding, gliding through the ether
Doing whatever, going wherever
Between life assignments – adrift
In limbo – grasping a reborn tether . . .
                                    (continues)

Through love
As a thought
Then an idea, a desire
An act of passion
A fertile solitary cell
In a warm and cozy dwell
So dark, tender, so serene
To grow in solemn innocence
Time capsule opens to guide
The traveler to another world

Suddenly, a burst of light
A slap - a cry – in wonder
Comfort stares
Loving shares
In a wonderful world
Cradled and curled
From a need to know
Then again to grow
What comes next?
Why, where, when, and how?

First, discoveries
Two eyes to see
Two ears to hear
A nose to smell
A tongue to taste
A touch to feel
Two arms to reach
Two hands to clutch
Toes to wiggle
Mouth to giggle
    (continues)

Then, choices
Too warm, too cold
From right to wrong
Too weak, too strong
To give and take
To sleep, to wake
Too sour, too sweet
To trick or treat
To love or hate
Too soon, too late

Then, questions
Why this, why that?
Where are we going?
Are we there yet?
Where do faeries come from?
Where do faeries go?
What holds the stars up?
What is a lie?
And if so; why?
Who is Santa Claus?
Why are there grandmas?

Then, without duress
Comes insightfulness
The sky is as blue as your eyes
Birdies are singing lullabies
Feel your heart go ta-tum, ta-tum
Tummy's growling; feeling bum
Love the animals, love the trees
Love to sit on grandpa's knees
Lovely roses smell heavenly grand
Yet bear thorns to hurt my tiny hand   (continues)

From tyke to teen to toil on or bust
Life on a roll with relish and must'
Seeking, groping for a proper rhyme
Hop on the bike tyke, enjoy the climb
Loping larva, comfy womb to butterfly
Life ever changing, not to wonder why
Think out of the box – beyond the nest
Solve the riddle – you've passed the test
Toiling yourself silly to be certainly able
To stop and reset time's reliant turntable

Words may be spoken – but never be heard
Sometimes real – sometimes totally absurd
Heed not innuendoes – stay with the dear
Believe in the future – there's nothing to fear
Walk out of your shadow – seek only light
Rainbows are arching – cherish the sight
Cosmic forces – rev up to full throttle
Dreams will flow freely – out of the bottle
Suns and moons - dancing with bright stars
Road bumps and hiccups – heal without scars

Sitting here like birds in a wilderness
Waiting for pursuit of your happiness
Some say wounds heal with passage of time
Some say lips squeal if a line doesn't rhyme
Hold tight onto this slick slippery slope
Nothing is left except for destiny's hope
Step right out with your head held high
Into the forested meadows up in the sky
Knowing full well that a gasping breath
Brings in new life before bringing in death
      (continues)

A body, thru an instinctive notion
Tends to stay in constant motion
A journey enjoyed
Like larvae deployed
Loving life, living love
A challenge, a push, a shove
Seeking something clear
Past is no longer here
For there comes a date to keep
Prepare yourself for the big sleep

A body at rest tends to stay at rest
No need to seek any other quest
Now a revelation comes to mind
For now, all shall be left behind
Strength of body stays right in here
Comfort reigns in a secluded sphere
Feel new worlds changing, drifting
Feel your body movements shifting
Now, as a pupa senses a new story
Bursting out into a grandiose glory

Pure excitement comes from within
As a third life stage is about to begin
Enlightenment streams into the sky
Joyful swoops and swirls flutter by
Born from a comfy cocoon curled
Future is now in a brave new world
From a recreation of a dream reborn
To hope rising high on a sunlit morn
From a spirited rapture soaring free
To a soul seeking tenure universally
      (continues)

Free souls – cosmic dust – adrift
Sliding, gliding, through the ether
Doing whatever, going wherever
Between life assignments – adrift
In limbo – grasping a reborn tether

How Novel

Minds in frenzied research
Swamped with data overload
Bogged in useless information
Expounding into great lengths
Releasing gnarling woven plots
Spun in confusion and intrigue
Incessant dialogs, rampant banter
Mirroring the frailness of humanity
When it comes to *"less is more"*
With fewer words and great insight
A poem brings forth a stronger bite

Creeping Out

Generating a thought by merely typing away
      Randomly hunt and pick in a whimsical way
Thought processes start with pardon-less nudges
      Erupting with smudges of deep rooted grudges
Inevitably there is always an outcome befalling
      Some semblance of terror as a demon is calling
Events disappear as idle thoughts silently die
      Then suddenly reappear with a blink of an eye
How odd life can be or even odder if it doesn't
      How weird is a mystery especially if it wasn't
From nonsense to all and all those outstanding
      To forests so awesome and seas so demanding
From trolls of droll drool and oodles of poodles
      To sinister secret codes and encrypted doodles
From minds in a clutter oozing slippery sputter
      To raunchy rats spilling from a gargoyle's gutter
From dragon cave lairs and teeth dripping meat
      To spiders, scorpions, and vile vampires in heat
From monster men in greed; wheeling and dealing
      To bad habits and hobbits or ogre-breath reeling
From prophesies, omens, and maidens held in keep
      To tingles, goose-bumps, and denizens of deep
From bogs and swamps; all while you are sleeping
      In your space from a place; crawlies are creeping

Author's Note

I have entered onto my writing tablet a disturbing discovery: Somehow my computer erased over eighty of my poetic endeavors written in these Chapters Fourteen and Fifteen. I may never see them again let alone remember what they were all about.

The Beginning

Chapter Fifteen:
Believing

I wish all the non-believers well.

PREFACE

Believing; how vast a word; and yet, how naïve. One can believe a lie, yet ignore the truth.

Remember in the New Testament when Jesus first proclaimed his Oneness with God. Most said he was a man; therefore how could he claim to be speaking the word of God? Even if he performed miracles; doubt still prevailed. What more could he do or say? He persisted and he repeated and repeated and still the people did not understand what he meant. And they were afraid. Most times the church elders remained skeptical and challenging. Their jealousy and fear kept their followers in check. The devil, the secret coach, skulked in the shadows, grinning all the while.

When seeking the truth, the difficulty occurs when finding what you think is real; may not be the truth at all. You have doubts as to it being believable. Acceptance is based entirely on faith – another vast, naïve word.

I chose "Believing" for the title of this Fifteenth Chapter because of the mystery (at least in this context) of what the word portends. One fact underlines all the rhetoric spoken and that is; something or some entity created what is all around and above us. We should be totally engrossed, in awe, enthralled, and reverent in respecting what is happening.

There is no greater thrill – so awesome!

In this chapter, I wrote the first poem "Escape" before I wrote this Preface.

Walk with me on this journey.

Enjoy the stroll.

Escape

Wander aimlessly out into the wilderness
Far from the scurry of the harried horde
    Be as one with the greatness of serenity
Where mere presence masks your being
Where you curl with the Book of Nature
    Reveling in the mysteries which unfold
Your new world comes pleasantly alive
Your sense keen to newborn wonders
    Abound in freedom as your aura glows
Only you possess the power to believe
Only you know today is not for naught
    For you've found the strength to go on

Crank It Up

Don't crank up the volume
    Of a rap-blaring boom-bass
Don't crank up the engine
    Of an ancient Model T Ford
Don't crank up the long handle
    Of a backyard water pump
Don't wake up in the morning
    A down-in-the-mouth crank
Do awake, feeling happy-go-lucky
    And crank up the day in glee

All in the Family

We all have heard about the age old story of the bitter feuding families of the Hatfield's and McCoy's;

>Boys versus boys
>Brothers vs. sisters
>Missus vs. misters
>Nephews vs. nieces

Well this next story is about two families living peacefully somewhere in nowhere called:

>the Bits and Pieces.

Venturing into dictionaries can be so much fun. The English language and the play on words will keep anyone happy and young for a long, long time.

Here is an exercise playing with words and having a 'pun' time doing it.

The Bits and Pieces

Once upon a time somewhere in nowhere was a little town called News. News was a kind of town where everything was little because everyone was little. Here was where the Bit family lived. The Bits were a rare, raucous, crazy, misfit family of characters.

The oldest was Tid who also happened to be the editor of the town newspaper called the Newsworthy.

If there was anything to say, Tid Bit would report it in full detail.   (continues)

The rest of the family of Bits was another matter. Including Tid; there were a total of eight. Listed here in no particular order are their names: Ra, O, Or, Ha. Hob, No, and Deb; - the seven dwarfs of News.

Ra Bit had a split personality. Either he was in a rage, foaming at the mouth; or he was a big eared critter hopping out of his magic hat.

O Bit was committed to his job and was inherently "dead to his writes".

Or Bit was the crazy nervous one, running around in circles, giggling gleefully all the while.

Ha Bit was in a rut doing the same thing every day while wearing her name on her head as she went off to church to pray.

Hob Bit was famous for he was the one who coveted the lord's ring.

Nob Bit was stuck to his brother, Hob Bit; for they were good buddies and inseparable; always hobnobbing around the town together.

Deb Bit was always behind and was the biggest loser of the family.

They all liked to get together and play the game of Alpha Bits. They were spellbound.

But there was another family who lived nearby in the town of Ate. The family's name was Piece. I'm sure you've heard of the Pieces of Ate.

Unfortunately, there was not much to tell. If one counted the pet monkey, there were eight in the family; Frontis, Time, Cod, A, Chess, Center, and Warren.

Frontis Piece is the leader who had spent his time starting all these tall tales.   (continues)

Time Piece was dialed in to his surroundings watching over everyone and everything.

Cod Piece was both a supporter and protector of all the private parts.

A Piece was a separatist, and was more inclined to remain as a reclusive kind of fellow.

Chess Piece was a game kind of guy who never mated but would jump if he had the chance.

Center Piece was narcissistic and demanded he sit on the center of the table in his full pompous regalia.

Warren Piece was a walking dichotomy going around hitting and kissing everyone and waging war peacefully; all at the same time.

The pet monkey's name was rhesus; Rhesus Piece was always lying around on the ground all over the town. Towns folk were constantly going around picking up rhesus Pieces. Ah, such was the slice of life.

Well there you have it. All you ever wanted to know about somewhere in nowhere. All this useless information came to you in bits and pieces. I am sure you just ate up all this juicy news

Waves of Light

Light waves streaming o'er the sand
      Sparkling bubbles dribbling
      Gathering, folding into mysteries
Retreating again into themselves
      Replicating the incessant journey
      Light moving, stimulating minds
Before and after humanity existed
      Darkness silently, showing no face
      Slithering into stunned nothingness
Light waves again streaming o'er the sand

Free Reign

A knight, - pounding thru his reign
Drenched, disheveled – pounding on
Rein free – fleet of foot – forever fled
He must ride, and so in earnest, rode
Thru the ever winding lonesome road
Thru the dale, head o'er heels he flew
To nowhere – the only place he knew
Night stalks the land, smothering the sun
There's nowhere to hide, - no place to run
Don't stifle thoughts – get out of the rain
Run thru the meadow – go do it again
Lift your head up right out of the sand
Claim your life – give yourself a hand
You are the master – you hold the rein
This is your land to command and reign
You are as free as a bird – free as the sea
Go follow your dream – go frolic – be free

About Writing

From this writer's point of view, there are three categories of writing style; Technical, Common, and Creative. All three can be juxtaposed into any of the other styles; however, keeping each separate is not required but generally preferred.

Technical writing, for example, is used in when writing textbooks, or in an attorney's arguments or briefs, in a doctor's or scientist's analysis, or in an architect's or engineer's construction specification package.

Common writing is better described as everyday writing, like diaries, essays, speeches, correspondence, debates, newspaper articles, reports, editorials, presentations, and in nonfiction discussions and dissertations.

Dialogues are common in many books read for entertainment. Some fictional novels naturally tend to drift into the third category.

Creative writing appears through imaginative, innovative, and inspirational efforts. Poetry, lyrics of musical compositions, plays, and novels are examples of creativity.

Creative writing is also free-thinking and explorative. Rules may be broken or skewed. The author will tend to prefer metaphors over similes.

Figures of speech such as personification, alliteration, and assonance are implemented freely without forcing their usage. The writer has empathy for the subject being written and senses the flow of its feelings.

(continues)

Grammatical rules are strictly enforced in novels or poems of prose; but are not as prevalent in musical lyrics or poetry of meter, rhyme, or free verse.

When writing in meter and/or rhyme, the verse should flow as freely as the music in the night, or as the sounds and rhythms of Nature, or as all pleasantries soothing to the ear. To do this effectively, one needs to get the message across in a concise way. Not an easy task, but if achieved, leaves the writer and the reader with a sense of satisfaction and gratification.

By the writer's tendency to not elaborate in great detail; the reader is encouraged to imagine feelings inferred. The reader uses these experiences to further imagine and explore in their own fashion' – thus drawing their own conclusions.

"Less is more" is a very effective adage to keep in mind when writing effectively.

* * * * *

Black Cloud Saloon at Thunder Gulch: A Tale of Yore

The name of this saloon sounds like an old western rooting tooting haunt where Piss-Pot Pete just might go looking for Cork Screw Sal. Or could it be a down trodden hangout for any ornery cuss like Dangerous Dan McGrew? Could it really be?

Could it happen?

(continues)

Off Route One in Florida sits a sprawling spread.
No crazy critters to rope, wrestle, brand, or dread
Stockades are revving up grunting hogs to ride
And dirty dust devils are thrown aside in stride.
Where hides, heads and horns adorn wooden walls
Where big round tables drape fancy oil cloths
Now comes the part that becomes intense
The part that brings Black Cloud portents
Reality into fantasy into fiction into lore
A story told like was never told before
A story that Begins and ends right here in Thunder Gulch
Hefty mugs of froth are drawn to lips unglued
Everyone is eyeing every other sleazy dude
Dancing is nothing; clones doing a prancing drawl
Even bar flies are drowning in the wonder of it all
When in strode a horrid oracle; Dirty Dick Dockery.
Skin looked as old as some ancient Greek crockery.
Tess and Jess, known as the Sinister Sisters Sludge,
Bold and bad; bearing some unfounded grudge
All three sidling in with a sleazy slithering stride
Three mighty mudslingers feared far and wide
The cacophonic crowd in silence stood entranced
Happy hearts, limber limbs ceased; no one danced
Little brown mouse crept back to his hole in the wall
Full moon glowed; hounds howled a mournful call
The world had stopped except for the unsavory three
Who strode to the bar to quaff one hundred – all free
Dirty Dick to the crowd said; "I've a story to tell.
So you all better listen before you all go to hell!"
      (continues)

Aboobenatum, tribal chief of the Klan Clan, increased his fold by ten when his beau bitch of late, Bessie Biglitter, bore forth a quintet of twins identical. The big Aboo immediately shouted that things were getting entirely too urban. So he therefore set forth his first decree in order to squelch the population explosion.

All female daughters
of the even numbered wives
(Later known as the DAR)
would avail themselves
to the Tribal Altar and
forthwith sacrifice their
maidenheads to the Tribal
Seamstress; Stitcher Snatch.

Aboo was certain he had his problems licked and all sewn up until his rebellious second spouse, Upenatum; weary of all this women suffrage, decided that, in order to get even; she pronounced a second decree.

All the male sons of the
odd numbered husbands
(later known as the Odd Fellows)
would avail themselves
to the Tribal Altar and
forthwith sacrifice their
manhood's to the Tribal
Cookie Cutter, Upenbitum.

(continues)

This was a tremendous blow to Aboo and all mankind. A furor emerged. The furor was embodied by Aboo's eldest oddest son of the now even second wife. His name was appropriately Adolph Not Gone Dong. Adolph, grasping his cherished fountainhead of youth, gathered all the even sons and odd daughters. Being a minority, they escaped by dashing across the "One Hundred Yard Meadow", the only secure haven in the Klan Clan Land. There lies the magnificent Peoples Tribal Bank. The future and the economy were now in the hands of these uprights. They nurtured, cultivated and molded the society that we have now all come to cherish today as the Great Society. The End.

The Black Cloud Saloon was in utter chaos. The once rapt crowd was now a frenzied gathering of sickening, snickering, slobbering laughter. A mad rush to the already jammed restrooms ensued. The Black Cloud UFO (Unidentified Floating Object) sailed Southward down Route #1 until it ran aground next to the White Eagle Lounge.

Bloody Mary anyone?

The First Anomaly

Strange
So different
Another world
Another time
Am I here?
Where is here?
Three moons grinning
Swirling, spinning
Purple sky
Orange mountains
Trees that fly
I lost my touch
No feeling on my fingertips
Is this real?
Pinch me someone
I am alone
Oh no! Wait!
Something wonderful this way comes
Curiously strange
Is it a bubbling mirage?
Or is it an illusive aberration?
As a soft breeze whispers
Flowing through me
And then gone
I feel wonderful, yet strange
Like I'm beside myself
Wandering in an alien presence
This must be a dream
What a great day!
Will tomorrow be any different?

The Second Anomaly

Strange
So different
A world I once knew
In a time I once was
I am here; but am I?
Yesterdays are gone
Tomorrows are yet to be
Is this land my land?
Or is it an island?
Green mountains
Blue skies
Trees so majestic
Serenity in bloom
I am alone
I can feel the green and the blue
I can breathe the trees
I can climb the mountain
I can feel the breeze
I am here
But where is here?
Oh, no! Wait!
Something wonderful this way comes
Strangely curious
Reality seeking truth
A soothing hush wafts over and thru me
I feel cleansed, warm, and comfy
I feel like I'm in heaven
Drifting as a cloud
For forever and a day
I hope tomorrow never comes

Play by Play

        The best part of a playground,
if you dare swing in one,
is to see beyond the saw
and slide through life's adventures
knowing there is more to fun
than going on a merry-go-round.

        Being bored is really a tired way
of looking at yourself.

        Tales play out short
when compared to the story of one's life

        A play on words is a play with words.

All about Ells

    Linger longer
    Leave later
    Loiter little
    Laugh lots
    Live large
    Lust less
    Love life

A Solemn Vow

Along the swirling pathway of dreams
Each step streams with colorful themes
Do not dare awaken; no, not right now
Continue to muse with a solemn vow
Come each dawn; blooms beam bright
Come each eve, eyes close for the night
To love – to cherish what nature brings
To protect – to save all precious things

Flights of Fire

Twinkling flits afire
Popping here and there
Blinking wisps inspire
Catch them if you dare

Fluttering in the night
Dancing n the dark
Winking oh so bright
A luminescent spark

Beckoning trysts in play
Rising up thru inky sky
Taunting the night away
Lovely wondrous firefly

Bred Crumbs

Though down and dirty
No need to clean this up
Born to live
Let them lay
Dreams are battered
Thoughts are scattered
Litter breeds in the fray
Loneliness strewn
Change not the tune

Off His Rocker; Out to Lunch

Everything's so hazy
Call me crazy
My mind is out to lunch
But I've got a hunch
So not to fret
Taint over yet
I'll relight my torch
Be out back rocking on my porch
Be there in just a little bit
I'll never quit
I will rock you
Until I bid adieu

Tale of Two Ditties

One Ditty One

It was out at the animals' fair
The birds and the bees were there
The monkey spiked the punch
Everyone had gone for lunch
All the big cats lagged behind
Crawling into everyone's mind
Screams startled the wily monk
One Ditty got exceedingly drunk

Two Ditty Two

Up in a tree sat the owl and the pussy cat
Sharing unwisely 'bout this and 'bout that
The owl threw a big tantrum out of the tree
While the pussy sat purring as calm as can be
The tree was befuddled; the sea turned to green
While the tantrum lay stoic; so calm and serene
Soon nonsense stepped in and scolded all four
Two Ditty now more happy than ever before

The Shopkeeper

The door swung open and I walked into a dark, musty, decrepit shop. No one was there to greet me. I called out, but no one answered.

Curiosity getting the best of me; I wander into a back room. The space was jam-packed solid with innumerable memorabilia and countless curiosities.

A hooded shadowy figure is huddled over a small desk, quill pen in hand, and scribbling away on parchment. The hooded body seems engrossed in some laborious task of writing in a flowery, gracefully flowing, sensuous cursive script.

I know not his name; nor his way of life. I have yet to see his face. As I am reading what the writer is revealing; I will relate his intentions to you.

He writes:

"Who am I?
Here I sit writing away.
I think I have nothing to say.
I have no inkling of who I am supposed to be.
I have been sitting here contemplating a long time; - thinking about what I should write about.
Should I write about the time of once?
I think not; for all that reverie is irrelevant and nonsensical.
It is but a stage preset in my life page.
I will relate what I am not.
I am not a puzzle with all the pieces strewn about as stars in the universe; waiting to be gathered and fit into reality from some non-existent fantasy.
I am not a figment of my imagination.
I am not a phantom before my eyes.
(continues)

My life is a story untold; yet told and retold.
I am not here to entertain me.
I am not here to befuddle me.
I am here because I am here.

But yet, I am the pulse; - the beat in the heart of eternity.
I am both guide and guardian of and by my destiny.
I am here at my command.
I am the protector of my future.
I am the keeper of all truths known unto me.
This shop is a reservoir of wisdom and knowledge.
I am the master of my whims and my foibles.
I am the director of my play.
I bear the burden of playing my own lead role.
My acts play out as they are meant to be or not.
I will prevail and I will not fail.

Who is this guy? He is freaking me out. I must see his face. OMG!

He has no face, no countenance; - he has no image! Yet he sits before me; cloaked in silence.

Just who do you think you are?

You still do not get it.
I see and believe that we are one and the same.
You are looking upon your own egotistical meager self.
We are merely having a conversation.
We are not gazing into mirrors or crystal balls.
Your life is in our hands.
Live it.
(continues)

I am livid.

Is this the time for me to pass out, go bonkers, or curl up and die? I guess it is the time for me to realize that either I have been had or saved.

My life is suddenly as clear as a bell and my future path is spread before my eyes. No matter who you are or where you're from or how enigmatic you may be, sir; I thank you.

Hello world!

As I leave to return to my universe; I notice a sign on the door with the following message written in that same wonderful script:

> *This shop is always open.*
> *Come in and visit anytime.*
> *Remember me in your dreams.*
> *Believe-you-me;*
> *it will be well worth your time.*

The Beginning

Chapter Sixteen:
Tomorrow's Dawn

I would like to dedicate this book to my wife, Shirley.
Endearment understood and realized
    Sometimes not verbalized
        Yet always in my mind
            In my life, in my love,
                and in my happiness.

PREFACE

The previous Chapter entitled "Believing" contained, in greater proportion, subjects that are more serious and darker in feeling.

This is not my true nature; for I am more of a happy-go-lucky kind of guy and a free-spirited thinker. I have ended every chapter with the words; "The beginning" because, to me there is no end.

The title of this, the Sixteenth Chapter is called "Tomorrow's Dawn" which represents an emerging beginning. The dawn of each day is such a wonderful happening; a refreshing start for the new day.

As a poet, writing anything creative can be a pleasant experience. However, whimsy is finicky, and the poet's mood can change in a heart beat. Days on end can cruise by without a verse being written. The poet feels totally frustrated, not knowing why or how his creativity has ceased. But, as with any creative soul, he plods on with the instinctive belief that the writing will return. And it does.

Mood is the prominent factor which determines the subject matter. Enthusiasm and energy provides tempo and style while determination and talent provides the quality and craftsmanship.

Dawn is one of the most common examples of an incentive impulse which could lead to the evolution of a poem.

I hope tomorrow's dawn will be a good one. Wish us luck.

> *"If you missed the dawn*
> *I made for you today; it does not matter.*
> *I will make you another one tomorrow."*
>
> God

Dawn

A rising body mutters a sigh
A world befalls its wary eye
Memories stretch and waken
Dreams inadvertently taken
Far from the civilized crowd
Encased in a cloaking shroud
Imagery fades from darkness
Nothing contains a likeness
Anticipation has withdrawn
Thru the evolution of dawn
Nothing escapes my being
For if I seek, I will be seeing
Gone goes yesterday's sorrow
Dawn dresses up for tomorrow

Time's presence was of the essence
  But during its acquiescence
    Armageddon played his hand

Coming from the Dark Side

Swirls of doubt permeated from the shroud
Of the slinking specter as it screamed aloud

Clouds of innuendoes shed tears of dread
As the ever living became the living dead

A world in chaos decimated the loving land
Weeping now drifted with the shifting sand

Heaven's only haven swung the gates awry
Time had finally come to make demons cry

Dawn brought the light on a glorious plate
Goodness brought love overpowering hate

Serenity brought in flowing heavenly grace
Calm brought peace bearing an angelic face

Cat Scanners
       Catacombs and Catapults
     Catastrophes and Catamarans
         Catalogues and Catafalques
     Catalysts and Cataclysms
         Cataracts and Catamounts
     Well, isn't that the Cat's meow!?

Lost in Conversation

Hello! You must be Miss Taken?
No I'm not, I am Miss Behaved
I see. Perhaps you are Miss Informed
No I'm not! So you must be Miss Taken?
I most certainly am not!
So where is Miss Taken?
She was never taken.
She was always Miss Begotten
No-No! Miss Begotten is verboten!
What a rotten thing to say!
Okay. Then where is Miss Begotten?
I just told you; she was Miss Understood and taken!
Miss Understood was never taken; she was carried.
OH! Who carried her?
Why I believe it was Miss Carriage.
I think I've been taken!
Or, am I Miss Taken?
    And Miss Informed, and Miss Understood?
How do we end this misfit conversation?
I don't know; ask Miss Fit.
Oh-no! Who's Miss Fit?
You're such a twit. Such a nitwit! I quit!

Tiger Lily

Roadside wild
Tiger lily grows
Sunshine yellows
As lovely as a rose
Back-dropped in green
As regal as a queen
Free to everyone
Surprise for the eyes
Solace for the wise

Thru a Looking Glass

I spy a new world of wonder
One whose fragrances are so enticing
    whose views so inviting
    whose echoes so intriguing
    whose memories so touching
    whose plate is so fulfilling
Senses are so magnified
    so splendid, so gratified
The largeness of life evolves
The panorama overwhelms
    the heart and salves the soul
There are no worries left
    only joy and happiness
And you know what?
The looking glass isn't even the least bit rosy

Creation As dawn awakens
A mind stirs
A pen in hand moves
And a line is written
A song is sung
A quilt is spun
Seeds are sowing
Clouds are growing
Problem solving
An orb revolving
A child is born
A flower blooms
Dreams fulfilled
Bridges span from near to far
Buildings scrape a higher star
Ah! The poetry of life
Moves on and on and on
Written words defy description
Until stirred by a muse's hand
Then a painted masterpiece
Reveals inner harmonic beauty
Peace permeates through the land

Poetry of Life

As a fanning Swallowtail patiently siphons up
The tasty nectar waiting in a yellow buttercup

As a cooing caring mother cradles and cuddles
Her loving child with a bubbling face - huddles
(continues)

As silent hushes in a carefree secluded glen
Beckons with whispers every now and then

As an emotion from a scenic stage plays out
To a wide-eyed crowd so rapt and so devout

As a chipmunk on haunches munches a tasty treat
Suddenly scampers away with adventuresome feet

As a silent, deft spider weaves its elegant web so fine
Crystal dewdrops hang as gems in dawning's shrine

As leaves of trees dance with parading clouds aloft
Cascade shadows mimic play on forest floor so soft

Thru the day, life plays on and lovingly oversees
All the tweeting birds, busy bees and happy families

Eventually comes twilight with moonlight so bright
A world stares awestruck in a haunting hush of night

Gentle breezes waft thru the nave of whispering trees
Reverence of the moment, calmed souls bent to knees

Then comes the lumbering giant of blissful slumber
An inducer of dreams and tales of a greater wonder

A new day and a new dawn brings in a new surprise
So with vim and with fervor, life opens up their eyes

Ideas dawn and spawn in exhilarating free fashion
Coming to fruition in a crescendo of pure passion

There is Always More to Learn

A youth, though innocent, through learning; gleans experience and confidence. As one grows older, confidence and experience melds into wisdom. But the wise person knows there is always more to learn.

Such a phenomenon is something like a false dawn. The real thing is coming, yet despite being close at hand, it is still not quite here. And even when it does begin to arrive, you know there is always more to learn.

Start with the little things. Larger understanding is built on the little things. Be patient and take nothing for granted; for sooner or later, everything will come together. All of a sudden the essence of your efforts dawns on you. Yet there is always more to learn.

A tiny pyramid sticking out of the earth sets a mind to thinking. Is there more to this than meets the eye? By digging deeper, the pyramid becomes larger.
When will it end; and what does it mean? There is always more to learn.

If you compose a poem that rhymes, yet has no subject matter; is that considered to be blank verse? Should we give it a try?

There is always more to learn.

Zero

Subject missing; nil to rehearse
Poem takes a turn for the verse
So nothing ventured; nothing gained
As thru a sieve; thoughts are strained
Input's slim; while output's lame
Nothing said; now that's a shame

Lonesome Trail

All alone
Musing
Walking
Leaving no footprints
Roaming into nowhere
Nothing right
Nothing left
Straight ahead
No place to go
No place to be
As it is above
So it is below
Horizon-less
Direction-less
Destination-less
Time-less
Through turmoil
Tempting
Tainting
Taunting
Why bother?
Time to stop
No!
Move on
Straight ahead
Keep your head
Keep your faith
Keep your life
Forever
Believe
Walk on; walk on.
When you are there
You will know

Here lies the Land of Ever

Cloud nine
Just up ahead
Nothing to dread
Wonders instead
Having never ever
Felt this way before
What do they want from me?
Nothing
They only want to give
Forever
And ever
Overwhelmed
Confused
Yet with a feeling of
Euphoria
Joy
Empathy
Utter bliss
With no remiss
Stepping forth
Without hesitation
Relieved
Resolved
Confident
Expectant
Reverent
Into the Land of Ever
Forever
Wow!

Avenue of Dreams

Something forever tempting this way comes
A Fair of Curiosities has arrived in your town
See the grizzly clown with the mystical frown
He who hides sinister things to bring you down

Barkers strut beneath banners so brilliant
Selling slimy sleaze; bad thoughts they sow
With a menagerie of fiery fantasies aglow
Choose any; then enter; enjoy their show

Wide-eyed gasps stare aghast and beguiled
Into a bedeviled world deep down under
You know you've made an errant blunder
As all earthly morals are now torn asunder

Your eyes are bathed by insidious decadence
Your brittle mind strains to curl and cower
Sensibility seeps into the deep boggy bower
As it succumbs to some greater alien power

Avenues of escape don't come to you easily
Don't gaze back upon an evil cryptic vault
Rush away now. Don't waver, turn, or halt
Lest you want to become a tall pillar of salt

Far from any dream you so well intended
Far from any avenue once travelled or not
Far from any stage that destiny might plot
Souls saved as those from the Family of Lot

Battle of Poetic Wits

Probing vibes are here within randomly disbursed
Perhaps unwarranted, unrelated, as well as cursed
Pleasant vibes likewise, herein readily interspersed
With vim, vigor, rhyme, or rigor, as well as versed
Happiness wins hands down over all the sadness
When all goodness outwits the hordes of badness
When evil stalks the caverns seeking unwary prey
A healthy mind wins with strength in every way

Picture This in Song

All that I am is about you
I see an aura all about you
There's nothing more I need to know
I need to know. I need to know.
Can't begin to know all about you
Out there on a far distant shore
I need to know. I need to know.
I need to know all about you
The lady in blue, dancing in tune
Here I am, I swoon under our moon
All that I care is about you
All that I own is about you
All that I am is about you
Dance with me then. Dance with me now.
Until the dawn breaks, thru all the heart aches
All that I am is about you
Beyond the end of our time
All that I am is about you
About you, about you
All that I am is about you

The Come-ons

Come to me, my humungous hunk
Come and partake this offering, my sweet
I'm the dream phantom of infinite enticement
Here to stir your alluring lips with excitement

Come to me, my luminescent lilac
Come and receive this myrrh, my honey
I'm the hummingbird of blissful happiness
Here to sip your aromatic nectar brightness

Come to me, my florescent firefly
Come enter into this offered web, my darling
I'm the fearless omnipresent light dream matcher
Here to entangle your body into my silky catcher

Come to me, my ever faithful filly
Come whinny here around me, my lovely
I'm the stalwart stallion of the fruited plain
Here to horse around and stampede you insane

Come to me, my sparkling secret star
Come lay your beams upon me, my mate
I'm the patient, dreamer, ever-watching soul
Here to inhale your ecstatic dream caresses whole

Come to me, my regal honey queen
Come enter our elixir garden, my delight
You who have exquisite love to elicit firepower
To ignite my bloom to burst into a loving flower

Star in My Pocket

So long ago
I caught
A fallen star
And saved it
Right here
In my pocket

One teary dreary day
Woes came
With crying rain
And tormenting pain
Dampened spirits
Enveloped me
Droplets of despair
Drenched me
Slowly, slowly
Reaching down
I withdrew the star
Slinging it away so far
Then, with a mighty <u>thwack</u>
 Of light and thunder
A new day of cheer and wonder
Exploded before my weary eyes
Overwhelmed and surprised
I ran as if there was no tomorrow
Leaving my cares behind
I leaped up high
And soared into the sky
Into the truth, into the light
Now all lovely and bright
No matter how hopeless
No matter how far
I <u>will</u> follow -
Follow that star

Liquid Mind

Slip, slip sliding away
Flowing to where
Senses are concealing
Thoughts are reeling
I'm losing the feeling
Slip, slip sliding away
Something isn't right

Once upon a time ago
I was taught to not only
See a rose, or hear a rose
Or feel, or touch a rose
But to smell the rose
Breathe. Inhale the aroma
And all will be right

In a time reborn
Regained senses
Flowing in here
Without any thought
Lessons are re-taught
I smell the rose
And all is right again

Clairvoyant Insight

Give us good logical reasons to wonder why
Our world is shifting slowly - running awry
Fear in the faces of concerned troubled souls
Outweighs hopes of what our dream unfolds
Give us the strength to upend what's wrong
Move forward as one strong universal throng

Transcendent Tendency

An urge so strong
Above all else
An urge to reach a star
And ride it far
Beyond comprehension
To go outside of this sphere
See the world anew
Take the A train
Beyond the horizon
Until all senses
Burst into clouds of wonderment
Never to settle nor meddle
With mediocrity
Invention without dimension
Imagine reality
As infinity in your hand
Releasing
A big bang event
Exploding revelations
Of new and exciting ideas
To enhance
The welfare of humanity
So let's begin
Above all else
With the urge so strong
For us to hitch a ride
On the rising star of imagination
Let us blow our minds wide open
And live as we've never lived before
Arriving in a new place in a new space
Where hopes and dreams we'll explore

The Arrival
Something new this way comes
We are here at last
Our time is now
Observe the view below
Here lies the beginning
Unburdened save for
Humanity in our cargo hold
We face a challenge unchallenged
An adventure too wonderful
Believing that the urge
Has now become a reality
Not a fantasy of our dreams
We believe that the why and how
Jump-starts our oneness now
With a scythe and a plow
We will till our brave new land
Till nature offers a helping hand

Remember
Bubbles burst in frenzied flight
Heed the hint - however slight
Hear the rustling of fallen leaves
Feel the gentleness of the breeze
See the blush that blossoms show
Even soft whispers of fallen snow
Feel the summer warmth again
With ever tingling drops of rain
Remember all the hush so splendor
Remember all your loves so tender
Flee no danger – belay your fright
May we dream our dream tonight?

Drifting

I am a carried whim
Flowing gently
Carefree
Whimsical
Bearing no burden
Bobbing wistfully
Thru sands of time
Sublime, dreamily
Fluffy clouds of delight
Never to alight
Lost in comfort
Gliding in thermals
I am neither here nor there
Just everywhere
As a flurry in no hurry
Just adrift
In a lazy way
Wafting away
Into a bliss
A blush –
A hush - a kiss
Into a pleasure
A wonderland –
An Eden - a treasure
Wherein dreams may come
And tarry
But never - ever fade away

Trendsetting

Each day our sun leaves the east horizon
Bestowing us a warm greeting of hello
Dare we yearn for something even better?
Dare we wish for some other greater show?
Some trends are meant to be seen forever
Some trends are meant to set hearts aglow

Every day our sun seeks the west horizon
Bringing forth great spectacles to behold
Dare we crave for something ever better?
Dare we hope for something else to unfold?
Some trends are meant to be seen forever
Some trends are meant to eternally be told

On the other hand, fads are passion driven
Fancies gleaned from madness of the horde
Dare we play the role for something better?
Dare we blindly follow those once adored?
Some fads will fail to ever become a trend
Some fads will fade by their own accord

Half a dozen crazy ditties coming your way next. . . -
Captain Marvel

Marvel me this, marvel me that
What the heck are we looking at?
Serve a verse or carve a crave
Twisted words are worth a save
Lines are written short and sweet
Enjoy. Listen. Please take a seat.

Danger Lurks

Just around a corner dark
An omen skulks in hungry gloom
Methinks I see a boogey man
An urge to lam – to another room

Another Time

Another time, another rhyme
Another day to while away
Another thought to prance and play
Another dawn to greet my day

Short Snorts

Wisp of breeze, flocks of fleas
Raging bull, nostrils wheeze
Stomping hoof, red eyes in rage
This line sets the second stage

I stand in fright, tense and tight
Bull will charge with super might
I, in haste, with full intent to flee
"This is a lot of bull. Oh, save me."

The Fifth of Four

Four little ditties came before this one here
Four little ditties neither quaint nor queer
All meant to amuse using nonsensical lore
This fifth is no different than the four before

Little Big Pause

Climbing over rocks
Scampering thru the trees
Strolling sands aside the sea
Especially when you're with me
For being together in this time
Over, thru, aside – all three
So cool; you surely must agree?

Vendetta

Two strangers in the evil dark
Out looking for each other
Two strangers in the ever dark
Seeking to destroy each other

How can strangers bear this hate?
Neither has the upper hand
How can strangers seek this fate?
Both take the stubborn stand

Seeds were sown in ages past
    Hate and fear bloom very fast
The race was lost from the start
    Good and evil doing their part
All the runners waited fidgety, at the gate
    The black, the white, the yellow, the red
The poor and wretched, the rich and blest
    Gods of peace, gods of war
Greed suppressers, power oppressors
    Lecturers of grief, prophets of doom
Humanity swept up by one humungous broom

To Amuse a Muse

My-my, oh my muse
How did you fare today?
Pray tell; what does amuse you?
How may I amuse you?
What if I dare to
Tickle your fancy? Whistle a whim?
Cradle a coo? Muster a moo?
Mime a rhyme? Lullaby a butterfly?
Where to begin?
I query your pleasure
In turn, you dwell in mine
Share me your wisdom
Justify me; inspire me; entrance me
It is I who wonders
You who sits and ponders
It is I who creates
You who sits and ruminates
It is I who delivers
You who hides in mirrors
Are you laughing yet?
Is your stoicism
Your only schism
You answer me not
Well, muse; thanks a lot
I guess, between you and me
I must do it all by myself

(Imagine that; it worked! I immediately created and wrote the following parable.)

The Feather and the Fern

This is a story about a feather and a fern. Duh!
They happened to be good friends and were very "frond" of one another. Yet they were entirely different. They met once again, when the feather had an "out-of-body" experience. He dropped in on the fern, living peacefully down below in his soft meadow-like domain.
The conversation went something like this:

Hi there Fern, how have you been? It took me ages to float down here. I broke loose in a skirmish with Hawk who won the battle. I have no regrets, nothing to crow about now!

Well, hi there Feather. It's nice that you dropped in. You are all black today; and so big. How did you wing that?

Oh, I was flapping a bit too much. Hawk kind of bit off more than he could chew. I cut loose and here I am!

Wow! That's exciting! Well there's nothing much happening here in the Fern Farm. We are all just growing and sweating all day and every day. Damn misting machine!

I envy you Fern. Your arms are so proper, green, and neat. You are well balanced about your central backbone. Your fronds are so tiny at the top and then they become so big when they get to the bottom. You are so structured, so compounded, and so intricately complex. You remind me of how the way that Spruce looks over yonder.

Yeah thanks; but I am not plump and fat like Spruce. I'm much smaller, flat, lean, lacy, and skinny. Look at you Feather! You got deep black fronds all on one side of your backbone. They are so fresh and silky-shiny looking.
(continues)

Your fronds all start big and get smaller towards the tip. Your outfit is much better than last month when you were a scrawny- frazzled grey, fuzzy snip.

Oh yeah; that was a hoot! Owl lost the tip of his tail in a tussle with Crow. I was ejected and totally blown away.

You sure have an interesting and varied lifestyle. I wish I had adventures like you have had. It must be neat to be up in the sky and flying about. You are so free!

Oh Fern don't wish that! I am separated from life and dying almost every day. You are alive and have a great life full of youth and you will grow up to be beautiful and graceful. You are so blessed.

Well, that's nice of you to say Feather. I never thought of myself that way. I guess I do live sort of a charmed, yet serene, life. Oh, my goodness! Here comes Man! He will see you and pick you up and throw you away. Quick; hide under me now! Oh! Too late! Wow!
Look; he stuck you in the brim of his hat! That looks cool Feather! You will see more of the world now, Feather. Bye; and good luck!

Bye Fern. I'll drop by again as another kind of spirit sometime soon. I'm happy now in this moment, and feel so important for I am a feather in this man's hat!

Both Feather and Fern went on to live productive full lives. They were each so happy knowing their value in life and realizing how important every little thing was to them.

P.S. Thank you Muse

The Genesis Conundrum

When does the beginning begin? Omega asked.
It begins when the end ends, Alpha answered.
O: *What is meant by: "the end ends"?*
A: *Everything ceases to be. Nothing exists; no movement, no light, no dark, no substance, no life, nothing.*
O: *Nothing. That is tough to imagine.*
A: *Right nothingness; - an absolute void.*
O: *So what about "the beginning begin"? What does that mean?*
A: *That means: the very instant that something evolves; comes into being, like altered states, movement, even life. Something just becomes, happens.*
O: *You mean like the Big Bang Theory?*
A: *Not necessarily; it could be the littlest of things. Like a micro-size movement. It is the essence of being, as a seed evolving.*
O: *Wow! Who witnesses this happening? Who knows?*
A: *Who does know? No one does. It could be rumor, fate, belief, maybe just faith.*
O: *That is utterly baffling! Isn't it?*
A: *Stupendously so!*
O: *So what do we do now?*
A: *Oh just about anything you want to do. You can ponder, dream, wonder, marvel, or meditate. You can write something about it. You can choose not to believe it. Or you can just plain forget about it.*
O: *Cheese! I'm overwhelmed, aren't you?*
A: *You bet! Imagine our universe and all that there is, is like an expanding meadow of wildflowers. Stars burst from new buds and then nurture other buds that will follow them. One day, a little earth-bud blooms then grows until it grows old and dies. Think about it.*

Changing of the Guard

Realms of Glory; Realms of Might
Pomp and Circumstance
Through Day and Night
Silent rituals rote in dance
      Save for muffled murmurs
      In cadenced motion
      Precision stomps
      Time sensitive notion
As sunset comes
Thru bustling crowds
The keepers of the night
Donned in shrouds
      As sunrise comes
      Tradition personified
      The keepers of the light
      Forever mollified
Change your guard
Hold your course
Security blanket
Presence in force

Breaking News

The end of humanity begins with the beginning of a new deal. He who does not heed this news alert may find himself in a new paradigm of thought.

According to previous information, the future of mankind depends on the premise that all men are created equal. This is no longer believed to be the case.

A secret society of powerful tyrants will soon rule the planet earth.

They do not come from outer space or the inner earth. They are an elite group of humankind who thrive on power, greed and indifference towards their fellow man. Mankind will become slaves of the new order and will be treated as such.

News Flash: a recent reader of this breaking news article was found seriously injured with multiple broken bones. He claimed he was running in panic after reading the article. He is recuperating in the local welfare insane asylum/hospice.

New News Flash: several people have died laughing in disbelief after reading the above News Flash.

Later Breaking News: Thousands of citizens all over the country are running away trying to escape slavery. Read the new books: Words in Chaos and Shutdown My Mouth by Texas warlord Theo Cruise.

Stay tuned to this station for updated information.

Final Breaking News: Heat generated by all the running, scraping soles, and escaping 'souls' caused the earth to begin burning! All is doomed. Goodnight and farewell.

Life of Day

Breaking dawn
Mowing lawn
Salmon spawn
Pale and wan
Boredom yawn
Sarah Vaughn?
Save the fawn
Beware the faun
Move your pawn
Where has everyone gone?
Bang the drums softly
Thru thick and thin
A song is about to begin:

> *Morning comes crisp and bright*
> *Flashing like silver*
> *Swift as the wild goose flies*
> *Dip, dip, and swing*
>
> *Soulful sounds swoon at night*
> *Leaves ply a shiver*
> *Eerie wails of the loon outcries*
> *Deep, deep, and sing*
>
> *Hearts do yearn however slight*
> *A time to deliver*
> *Keep all safe till dawn's reprise*
> *Sleep, sleep, sweet thing*

"I've grown accustomed to her face
　　She's second nature to me now"
　　　From the play, <u>My Fair Lady</u>

Three Times a Lady

She sidled up to my side
Glancing a tinkling winking eye
On my hand, her lips hushed a sigh
Then discreetly; her curtsy did implore

Escaping to the upper room
Embracing an alluring vivacious hue
On my command, her clothes she threw
Then lithely; she held her hands before

I screamed in a strange falsetto
How dare you disgrace my quarters so?
She said. *"Dear Lord; Please save my soul!"*
Then so sweetly, genuflected to the floor

As I flustered, twilight waning
I reached down to offer her all I bore
She remained unsure what was in store
Then hastily left, closing the chamber door

As I stood there wan and vacant
I reflected on events that left me hanging
Of escapades that had my head banging
Longingly, I pined for my lady even more

Warped Wit

When a wayward wind wallows
In the dungeon wakes of despair
Sure as shooting what follows
Is a biting, grimacing icy stare
Literacy and lunacy languish
Overcome with alliteration
Anguish struggles
And somehow survives
Epochal epitomes erupt
Intellect interludes; insanity intrudes
Astride with some foreign bride
Decadence dances far and wide
Wit wallows, ever waiting
Waiting, wanton, and wild
Spooked by insanity
Intrigued by vanity
Churned butter burned
Spurned tables turned
Till time tanks -
Will consciousness wait?
Will caution intervene?
How to proceed; how to succeed?
Space warps in time
Time stands silent,
Still until when,
Wit with a will
Saves the frigging day
Somehow, someway
Wit outwits mayhem
Plies, persists, perseveres
Free of life's deleterious debris
Warped, wily, and wheeling free

Contemplation of the Little Things

When in doubt; go space out
Into the forever out there
Rampant thoughts abound
Everywhere out there
Sunning themselves
Airing differences
Settling into coexistence
Do diligence
Big things tend
To somehow disappear
Problems solved
Again for another year
        However, little thoughts
        Tend to stick around
        Nagging the craw
        Little riddles with legs
        Fuzzy puzzles sprawling
        Mighty mites of mystery
        Noggin scratchers all
        Can't seem to reach
        Those itchy buggers
        In the middle of my back
        Can't seem to teach
        Them a thing or two
Mighty mountains
From little molehills grow
Allowing your mind to drift away
Tend to the little things
First thing every morning
You will see your troubles lift away
Into the forever out there

Isn't it odd; when thinking things, odd thoughts, most of the time, evolve?

Odds-on Favorite

What is your favorite thing?
If you are narcissistic, it would be love of self
If you are romantic, it would be love of life
If you are materialistic, it would be love of things
If you are selfish, it would be love of money
If you are antagonistic, it would be love of war
If you are pacifistic, it would be love of peace
If you are patriotic, it would be love of country
If you are poetic, it would be love well versed
If your are angelic, it would be love of God
We could go on and on
We seem to sense a pattern here; one of love
So what or who, or what, do you love the most?
What are the odds of guessing it right?
What is your favorite thing?
If you are lucky, it would be love of gambling
Don't bet on it!

Buckets of Charm

An interpretation of the lore:

Jumping Jack laboring at the still
Every day, many buckets to fill
Every day, up and down the hill
With the where-with-all and will
Carrying buckets down to the mill

Jumping Jack played many types of roles
His shoes were worn, his socks had holes
His feet were tired, his legs - stiff poles
His whole body ached, he had no goals
A life lived for whom the bell never tolls

Jumping Jack had the knack to settle his affairs
He went to school to learn to suppress swears
Learning that charm brought forth lovely stares
Now buckets no longer carried woes and cares
His charm broke the spell; catching Jill unawares

Explanation of the interpretation:

Jack and Jill were very much in love with one another
When Jack fell down; his 'crown' was not his head
His crown was his pride which was hurt a bit instead
Jill "came tumbling after" meant "fell head over heels"
Just shows you how a metaphor devilishly conceals
And yet how enigmatically and eloquently it reveals

Impact

Do words leap off the page to splat upon your face?
Or do they sink into debris lying in dumpster space?

Do spend time discovering clumps of jasmine blue
Or go climb up the wall just as monkeys like to do

Whenever your mindset dallies, just let it dangle free
Let the silly monsters hide in jars rather here with me

Muster all the bumblebees to buzz around the hive
Or muster all the bums of booze to rumble in a dive

When and if you stop composing some simple poetry
Remember all the rime that tumbled from your reverie

Remember how words dribbled forth ever pleasantly
For life enjoyed impacting with a merry muse like me

A Nutty Anecdote

"Gather your nuts while ye can.
You never know when the man
Will come to take you from this
Unusual doings with your miss,"

That's a quip from the squirrel
Whose bushy tail is in a whirl
If your mind unfurls; your nuts
Will go too; no ifs, ands or buts

"Double, double; toil and trouble.;
    Fire burn and cauldron bubble."
        From Shakespeare's Hamlet

What's Brewing?

What it is; is what it's not
Something is in that bubbling pot
See it squirming; see it shimmy
Damn if it doesn't look like Jimmy
What to do? It's awfully hot
Can't tell if he's alive or what
Stamp the fire – put it out!
Hurry, hurry; dump the pot!
Hey there Jimmy; you okay?
Little bit cooked; I would say
And then Jimmy up and spoke
And ever so blithely; he did invoke:
    "You dumb bloke, you crazy fool!
    I was basking in my hot tub pool!"
    Now look at me with all this mud;
    All covered with ash and other crud.
    Besides, the pot was filled to the brim
    With a pale ale brew to keep me trim.
    How am I going to get nice and prim?"
Here is the time when the writer comes clean
For it's up to the reader to conclude this scene
This is not really a cop-out, (Well, maybe it is)
As the writer, you have the power to be the wiz
I am just too hot, frazzled, and bothered right now
You will figure it out soon. I'm sure, somehow.
Ta-Ta!

Merely Talking

We are what we are and always should be
Grains of salt should be as they should be

Heavens are most becoming to all who care
Enter without sin and believe as you swear

Outcomes are incomes if they turn out okay
Believe in yourself, 'tis always the best way

Enter a labyrinth and exit profoundly amazed
Enter a maze and exit neither puzzled nor crazed

When in a house of mirrors and the floor is wood
Follow the plank lines and emerge as you should

What would it be like to be in heaven's back yard?
Strolling thru the grandeur of His green boulevard?

Created as equals; yet we hate more than we love
Why can't we live together as we shall up above?

God created kindness, empathy, heaven, and ethics
Devil created hatred, indifference, hell and pathetics

If one starts some task; not knowing of its outcome
Have faith in oneself; something good will become

The Worth in Looking Up

As the lights go out in my room, psychedelic images appear on the ceiling. As I stare from my comfy place in bed; conscience making day dreams are spreading panoramic images above. I lie mesmerized; embracing the spectacle with wandering wide eyed awe. There is no conceivable explanation for the visages above me, save for the tricks of light provoking the tapestry-like display.

Before I have an opportunity to analyze the artwork, it all fades from my view. I have only the next night and subsequent others to further study this fascinating phenomenon. I feel as if I'm viewing an instant Michelangelo mural on the ceiling of the Sistine Chapel.

Perhaps my three eye surgeries; two for insertion of pressure reducing stents in each eye, and one for a new cataract replacement lens in my right eye just might shed some light on the subject. (There is no pun intended here. Well, maybe there is just a tad.)

In two days I will have cataract surgery in my left eye which I'm looking forward towards the outcome. A continued show of a ceiling aurora borealis upon the completion of the surgery will be awesome.

Describing the colors, patterns, and intricate complexity encompassing the wonder may be difficult; but I will do my best to explain. A light blue-white background haze silhouettes black vines with petals, flowers, branches, and leaves of all shapes and sizes which trace an intricately complex intertwining stretched across the entire scope of vision. The scene is eerie, yet
(continues)

intriguing; simple, yet complex; and reminds me of the view seen of a forest canopy as one looks toward the sky; or of a biosphere-like botanical garden running wild.

It is a non-moving, static wonder staring back into my feasting eyes. There is always worth in looking up; yet the occurrence which is happening is on the fringe of a revelation that sets my mind to pose a query: "What's up Doc?"

The mind is like a pixie; always playing tricks and having enjoyment in performing them. Will we ever know just how much we don't know? Actually, I really don't care; for the fun of life is the unexplainable and wonderful events that happen almost every day and every night.

Stay young my friends and enjoy your journey of life on earth! Here's to you and here's to me!
Things are always looking up; and everything is well worth our time spent here.

Fringe I am standing on the edge of a revelation
On the precipice of endearing thoughts
On the brink of some outstanding event
Content in my demeanor; calm in my being
Ever mindful of my delicate surroundings
Ever careful of my ability to create dreams
Ever intrigued with the happiness of life
I am standing on the edge of preservation
What I say and do is in my humble realm
I have the courage and wisdom to survive

From the spark came the fire
From the fire came the light
From the light came the life
From the life came the love
From the love came the **Time Reborn**

The true happening emerged as the bellows
Breathed into the fire of desire and ignited
The spark that scorched away her dreams
She stood bewildered with a frenzied frown
Struggling toward the edge of her despair
She wept until her eyes melted to pools of oil
With nowhere to go and nothing to live for
She fled to the sanctum corner in her heart

He stood tall, strong, yet with wise intention
Grasping the bellows and snuffing out the fire
His regal crown lifted her ever- sparkling desire
Rekindling her dreams away from her sorrows
He tenderly caressed and freed her weeping eyes
As the pools of oil disappeared into the deep below
With everywhere to go and everything to live for
He glided into the sanctum corner of her heart

A bonding love grew exponentially stronger
As an exploding star blossomed in their midst
Together emerging as a living breathing nova
Together dwelling in everlasting universal bliss
Two loves would live as legend in ever-ever land
Two loves would seal all the bonds forever more
All would gather round praising the loving two
Entwined forever and ever in one another's heart

Eye Do   Surgery day
Last of four
Open wide
Stand aside
Eyes refreshed
Time to soar
Ready to roar
Gone the night
See the light
Love the day
In every way
Eye do, eye do, eye do

Alone   In the silence of the forest
In the chambers of a dream
With a waking waft of wisdom
Walk beside the swishing stream
Smell the freshness, sense the fervor
Taste the flavor, let it savor
Yet as I beg and as I plead
You beside me is all I need
Join me now on this our journey
Walk with me; memories free
Ne'er forget our idyllic spot
Stay forever; remember me

Much ado about nothing

Frivolous frequent fits of frenzy
Tantalize trying tainted troubles
Quibbling quotes quake quickly
While weak word warriors wail

"Power tends to corrupt, and
  Absolute power corrupts absolutely "
Lord Acton

"Power, like a desolate pestilence;
Pollutes whatever it touches; and obedience,
Bane of all genius, virtue, freedom, truth,
Makes slaves of men, and of the human frame"

"The awful shadow of some unseen Power
Floats though unseen among us – visiting
This vagrant world with an inconsistent wing
As summer winds that creep from flower to flower"
Shelley

Unknown Unseen

Money, Power, Greed; all three
The driving forces meant to be
Unknown, Unseen
Mountain movers, mind manipulators
Who kiss the eyes and alter the vision
Who manipulate the new dream weavers
Who command at the head of long tables
Rather than planning together in the round
Be wary of their dynamics and control
Be firm, yet gentle;
Be dogmatic, yet understanding;
Be resolute, yet thankful;
Be protective, yet flexible
Be tactful, yet embracing
Above all, remember your mission
Hold steadfast to your vision
Sustained by a sound foundation

Big Thoughts, Little Ponders

Hear the soft refrain of gently falling rain

See the moon in wane thru a window pane

Observe a croaking toad in a musing mode

Wander a mountain road to a quaint abode

Dawn brings surprises when the sun arises

Find a lesson learned from a talent earned

Would I be in trouble if I burst your bubble?

What's the Use?

We've certainly become a stagnant nation
With politicians' overly intense animation
Serving no substance, no purpose, or cause
Focus consists mainly on tea-bagger's jaws,
Shutdowns, filibusters, and party faux pas,
Ever looking busy citing other men's flaws

Protocol

By the way, Proto called me just the other day
He wanted to go to the church to sit and pray
I couldn't say; "No, I have other things to do"
I politely agreed and sat beside him in his pew
His demeanor sports a finely tuned decorum
Sitting there so proper; a rotund stumble bum
Customarily, I would be a thousand miles away
But today my weakness left my mind in disarray
Proto is eccentric and he is an elder of his church
I cannot go on pretending, defending or besmirch
I know Proto's type; he's a hypocrite and a sleaze
For he will cut you down if you so much as sneeze
He rules his mini-world like a tyrant on a wheel
When you're kind to him; your heart, he will steal
He takes your time away from you forever and a day
When it comes to Proto calls, 'tis best you stay away

I just had a conversation with Mother Nature and she handed me these next three poems:

Nature Calling

There is a briar in the bramble
And if you're prone to gamble
Blow your horn and a scorn will be led away

There are crickets in the thicket
And if you have a season ticket
Toot your flute and join the sensuous display

Oodles of frogs are in the bogs
Squatting atop the mossy logs
As they gloat and croak the entire night away

A swallow singing in the hollow
Bends a mind to seek and follow
An entrancing tweet dancing in a soulful way

There's hocus-pocus in the crocus
Peek in very closely; strive to focus
See the pixies romp and stomp in gleeful play

No errors appear in nature's wonders
No mistakes and certainly no blunders
Just lots of singing bringing joy to another day

Something to Blow Your Mind

She rose with a throbbing horrid headache
Blowing through the caverns in her mind
Raging torrents of dread curdled her blood
A restless rogue blew through her face
      Out into a cause torn asunder
Smacking head-on into a wayward wind
      Out into the world to plunder

How would she survive this ungodly blast?
How would she stop this ghastly overcast?

Pelted with rampant, raucous, shattered thoughts
She staggered aimlessly into the seething frenzy
Seeking only solace for her ravaged, savaged soul
Seeking only to secure a haven
      For her huddling, cuddling nest
She, a protective, motherly, saintly woman
      Living, loving her coveted quest

She is known affectionately as Mother Nature
She cuddled and coddled the wayward wind
She cradled and caressed the restless rogue
Until they settled softly into a gentle whisper
      Soothing, calmly, into a great beyond
These two breezy pals, swirling in ecstasy
      Plowing ripples across a golden pond

"The hills are alive with the sound of music."
From the Sound of Music

Rhapsody Arboreal

Mountains singing in the rain
Valleys echo the sweet refrain
Sing out hilltops, once again
Sing out!   Sing to me!   Sing!

An orchestra primed to fling
Instruments tuned to spring
A baton introduces the beat
Momentum surges to respond
To rhythm overtures beyond
As the breeze flows in so free
The trees stretch and awaken
Eyes in rapt and minds in awe
Anticipating an etude waterfall
Treetops sway and, in sky, play
Flowers dip, curtsy, and dance
Across a billowing lea expanse
Springboks soar in graceful arcs
Crickets chatter amidst the barks
Leaves of grass with tassels high
Sashay in unison, their voices cry
A menagerie of notes and ruffles
Sprinkling dews and soft truffles
Cavort as children filled with glee
The world has gathered just to see
A regal collaboration of nature's kin
And all the love found there within

So What's Becoming

When I endeavor to be clever
The weird emanations evolve
From somewhere deep inside
Something waiting to cry out
Wanting to scream and shout
I scream from the tallest tree
"So now what did become of me?"

When I discover what I uncover
Inside opens up to have a look
The outside reads like a book
A book that tells a boring story
Almost like an ancient allegory
I scream from the tallest tree
 "So now what has become of me?"

When undercover, I discover
That I still am one body whole
Protecting my ever wary soul
My soul tells me to stay kind
Keep ever sound of your mind
I scream from the tallest tree
"So now what will become of me?"

Written in Oblivion

When in oblivion
      try to imagine enigmatic mazes
While laboriously
      writing awfully weird phrases
Everything might be trite
      or maybe not really quite right
A mind out of sorts
      retorts as a high spirited sprite
Gardens resplendent
      with quilted, soft fluffy spreads
Turn wheedling queens
      with weep nodding heads
From giggling gossips
      with innuendoes implored
Into cracking their joints
      as they bother the bored
From silver linings climbing
      out of ivy twilled shawls
Who delve in dungeons dread
      where an ugly thing crawls
Liquid gold yearnings
      drip in sweet syrupy thongs
While sick stolen rights
      tumble into terrible wrongs
These hookah hyped verses
      twist curls into bubbling bongs
As this dream of an idiot
      remains right where it belongs

Man of Wit

> "<u>Mark</u> my words; the <u>twain</u> I shall I never meet."
> **James L. Harter Sr.** in honor of
> Samuel Langhorne Clemens

Man of wit
Writing as the alias,
Mark Twain
Not hidden
Not one least bit
One whom I never met
Except in verse
Yet, no need to fret
Wisdom may precede wit
Ah, but here's the rub
Wit lasts much longer
If you're a member of the club

Upstart

Creeping, leaping up from the floor
Thrashing, gnashing ne'er as before
Burning, yearning as the day breaks
Learning begins as early dawn wakes

Telling Tall Tales

A tall tale once told twice is told once too often. However, a tall tale never told is obviously never told until told once.

Once upon a time, there was a fair young maiden who was lovely, lithe, and loving. Her name just happened to be Belle. Belle tolled the town bell every morning, noon and night. She was faithful to the task and the town went about their business as any normal day in the town of Normal. Townsfolk relied on the bell being tolled for their daily routine centered about this timely reminder.

One day she missed her calling in the morning; and the townsfolk never woke up until she tolled at noon. Everyone was none the wiser. Midday breakfast completed, the folk went about their morning chores during the afternoon. They ate their lunch at supper and continued their afternoon chores during the night until Belle tolled the bell twice. Totally confused, the discombobulated crowd wandered about the town not knowing what in the world to do.

Meanwhile, the fair young, lovely, lithe, and loving maiden was also very much distraught. She had no idea how to fix the problem. Thinking all was for naught, Belle promptly rang the tolling bell in a strange melodious rhythm, varying the sounds appealingly thru the whole night and every night thereafter.

The reader is now wondering how this tale will end and the writer is wondering the very same thing. Telling tall tales is like telling little white lies but with a smile and a smirk that only gnomes can fathom.

(continues)

Normal townsfolk fell asleep standing up, while eating breakfast, lunch, and supper all at the same time. Then they all stood around playing, singing, partying all through the day. All was no longer normal in Normal. Everyone knew that Belle tolled the bell for them. They were so happy singing and playing; all the while listening to the bell tolls by Belle. But alas, there were no chores done, no work, all play, nothing normal, no town, except for the town's name which remained the same, - Normal.

But, just like in all tall tales told; everyone lived happily ever after. And just like in all tall tales; there is a moral. If you know for whom the Belle tolls; then you know that you will always be happy and live happily ever after. And so they did.

I trust we are all now very happy and will remain so forever after.

Fester Benders

Snickering bickering loathsome twit
Pestering, festering won't ever quit
I can't seem to escape one least bit
The spider web now has me in a snit

There's a fly in the ointment, oh so thick
Squirming, worming, fetch me a stick
Get it out, snatch it out, oh so quick
Ointment turned rancid. I am so sick

Out of the caverns, higher and higher
Dragons, in flight, spitting very hot fire
A world in chaos, thru dark muck and mire
The time is right now to sing hymns in a choir

Whittle Awhile Away

I used to whittle a little during my early life
Picked any old limb and with my pocket knife
Whittled a hiking stick; my name carved on it
Many times used in hiking, strolling quite a bit
I still have that stick, stored away somewhere
Along side late brother, Dave's whittled stick
In my cabin in the woods where sometimes I
Go to just sit and remember those other years
When I spent time with many now long gone
Leaving many memories of times spent in fun
While away the hours long past the setting sun
But yet those are good passing dreams of yore
For remembering is a lonely, but comfy chore

A Path Once Taken

There are many paths to take in life
The path of least resistance
Is the favorite one by far
Many trails are never travelled
Some say: "*Those are forbidden.*
Take only these I hand you now
Travel at your leisure
At your whim
But travel only these."
Why not those others?
What destiny lies over those horizons?
What mysteries are there to seek?
"Forbidden" as a word is a buzz
Temptation is the magnet speak
Unknowns – dark, danger, fear
But what is there to fear?
Nothing to fear but fear itself
All is within imagination's reach
Enter bravely – be the pioneer
Confront your destiny
Tread the pathway boldly
Our faithful sun lights the way
Leave the past – go into the future
Our presence is secure
Each step taken breeds experience
Any future steps breed confidence
On-the-job training and learning
Now! Look all around you. Wow!
Look there, and there, - everywhere!
See!   Look and see; really see! (continues)

Standing in the midst of revelations
In the discovery of new expectations
Drift thru rainbows of many hues
Slip thru waterfalls of wonder
Skim over rivers of rapture
Scamper up mountains of majesties
Stroll along limitless avenues galore
So much to see
Rubber-necking every which way
Opening cabinets of curiosities
So many adventures to explore
So much more than
What dreams are made of
Seems as if we are born again
All too wonderful, too grand
A path once taken
Is not a forbidden one
Nor a bothersome burden
But one of understanding
The mind is the path
The path is the knowledge
The knowledge is the key
The key opens a life lived full
To the brim and then some
Look here is another path!
Greeting us, inviting us
Into another beginning

Shall we go on? *"Let's go!"*
I'm excited! *"I am too!"*
Life is great, isn't it? *"Oh my, yes. Will it ever end?"*
Not in my backyard. *"Neither in mine."*

Demise of Conversation

He said she said nothing to him
She said he said nothing to her
Silence prevailed
Nothing further was said
Who the hell is relaying us with this?
Since nothing further is said; -
Why is there even a narrator?
This narrator sucks
Impeach him!
Silence is golden
It is as quiet as a church mouse now
Who said that?
Do we have another narrator?
Off with his head!
Narrators don't come cheap nowadays
Off with their heads!
There is a shutdown in congress
Off with all their freaking heads!
Off with <u>your</u> head!
Off with my hea . . . !

Just Words

Without a doubt, words expressed honestly,
    merit impartial and honorable responses.
In turn, responses simply put; reflect in kind, respect
    for those words so faultlessly expressed.

Tomorrow's Gift

We hope for a magnificent tomorrow
Dreams will have been thus perceived
When emerging dawn greets the day
We have faith that it will be achieved

There is no greater gift ever given
Nor any other we've ever conceived
For that love so elegantly reassured
Comes with enduring care received

Shall we go on?
　　　　　　　Let's go!

The Beginning

www.ingramcontent.com/pod-product-compliance
Lightning Source LLC
Chambersburg PA
CBHW071627080526
44588CB00010B/1298